100 PREHISTORIC ANIMALS FROM A TO Z

By Dr. Richard Moody

Illustrated by Paula Chasty

*Based on an idea by Ron Wilson
Prepared with the cooperation of Dr. Paul C. Sereno,
Department of Anatomy,
University of Chicago*

Publishers • GROSSET & DUNLAP • New York
A member of The Putnam Publishing Group

Copyright © 1988 by Patrick Hawkey Publishing Limited.
All rights reserved. First published in the United States
in 1988 by Grosset & Dunlap, Inc.,
a member of The Putnam Publishing Group, New York.
Published simultaneously in Canada. Printed in Belgium.
Library of Congress Catalog Number: 87-82490
ISBN 0-448-19071-0
A B C D E F G H I J

Edited and designed by Curtis Garratt Limited.

Contents

Alticamelus 6
Andrewsarchus 6
Archaeopteryx 7
Archelon 7
Arsinoitherium 8
Australopithecus 8

Baluchitherium 9
Basilosaurus 9
Brontotherium 10

Cheirolepis 10
Coelodonta 11
Crytoclidus 11
Cynognathus 12

Deinotherium 12
Deltatheridium 13
Desmostylus 13
Dicrocerus 14
Dimetrodon 14
Dimorphodon 15
Diplocaulus 15
Diplovertebron 16
Diprotodon 16
Dipterus 16
Drepanaspis 17
Dunkleosteus 17

Edaphosaurus 18
Elasmotherium 18
Eryops 19
Eunotosaurus 20
Eusthenopteron 20

Gerrothorax 21
Glyptodon 21
Gomphotherium 22

Hemicyclaspis 22
Hesperornis 23
Hipparion 23
Homo erectus 24
Hylonomus 24
Hyracodon 25

Hyracotherium 25

Ichthyornis 26
Ichthyosaurus 26
Ichthyostega 27
Indricotherium 27

Lystrosaurus 28

Machairodus 28
Macrauchenia 29
Mammuthus 29
Mammuthus
  primigenius 30
Mandasuchus 30
Mastodon 31
Mastodonsaurus 31
Megalichthys 32
Megaloceros 32
Megatherium 33
Megazostrodon 33
Merychippus 34
Mesohippus 34
Mesosaurus 35
Metacheiromys 35
Metamynodon 36
Microbrachis 36
Mixosaurus 37
Moeritherium 37
Mosasaurus 38

Neanderthal man 38
Neobatrachus 39
Nothosaurus 39

Ophiderpeton 40
Osteolepis 40
Oxyaena 41

Palaeolagus 41
Palaeomeryx 42
Panthera spelaea 42
Paranthropus robustus 43
Peloneustes 43
Phenacodus 44

Pholidogaster 44
Phororhacos 45
Placochelys 45
Placodus 46
Platybelodon 46
Plesiosaurus 47
Pleuracanthus 47
Procoptodon 48
Proganochelys 48
Protosiren 49
Protosuchus 49
Pteranodon 50
Pterichthyodes 50
Pteroplax 51
Pyrotherium 51

Quetzalcoatlus 52

Ramapithecus 52
Rhamphorhynchus 53

Saltoposuchus 53
Scutosaurus 54
Seymouria 54
Sivatherium 55
Smilodon 55
Stenaulorhynchus 56
Steneosaurus 56

Tanystropheus 57
Thylacocinus 57
Thylacosmilus 58
Toxodon 58
Triconodon 59
Trogonotherium 59
Tylosaurus 60

Uintatherium 60
Ursus spelaeus 61

Zalambdalestes 61

Animal History 62

A

Alticamelus

Alticamelus was a long-necked camel that lived in North America about 20 million years ago. It stood 10 feet (3 meters) tall and grazed on leaves from trees. With its long neck and legs and narrow snout, *Alticamelus* resembled a giraffe.

Like modern camels, giraffes, sheep, and some other mammals, *Alticamelus* was a ruminant ungulate (hoofed animal). A ruminant has an even number of toes on its split hooves and chews its cud. Slightly chewed food, stored in one of three or four stomach areas, gets softened into masses called cuds. The cuds pass back to the mouth and are mixed with saliva and chewed again. Then they are returned to the stomach for more digestion.

Ruminants such as *Alticamelus* must have found ideal the open edges of woodlands and the broad grasslands of ancient North America.

Weight: Not known
Height: 10 feet (3 meters)
Found: North America
Lived: Miocene

Alticamelus

Andrewsarchus

The large doglike *Andrewsarchus* was a distant relative of *Alticamelus* even though it was neither a ruminant nor even a hoofed mammal. *Andrewsarchus* and its immediate relatives appeared approximately 45 million years ago, during the Eocene Epoch. Smaller ancestors can be traced back into the Paleocene (54-65 million years ago).

Few details about the body of *Andrewsarchus* are known, but it was most likely quite long and heavily built. Its head measured nearly three feet (1 meter) long, and its flattened cheek teeth were probably used to crush bones. For, unlike most of its even-toed relatives, it fed on both plants and flesh.

Andrewsarchus

Scientists believe that *Andrewsarchus* hunted in packs and was able to outrun the large plant-eaters that it killed for food. In contrast to the hoofed animals, it ran on its fingers and toes rather than on the flat part of the hand or foot. Because of its size and weight, *Andrewsarchus* probably rushed at its prey in the way that a large bear does.

Weight: Not known
Height: 13 feet (4 meters)
Found: Asia
Lived: Eocene

A

Archaeopteryx

Archaeopteryx

"Ancient wing" is the common name for the first bird. *Archaeopteryx* lived during the Late Jurassic Period – as early as 140 million years ago – in what is now southern Germany. Only five fossils of this bird have been discovered. Three well-preserved examples, however – now stored in London, Berlin, and Eichstätt, West Germany – show the close links between dinosaurs and birds.

Archaeopteryx had feathers on its wings and tail. It had beaklike jaws as well as the small pointed teeth of its reptilian cousins. Three clawed fingers jutted from the leading edge of its wings, and three long-clawed toes extended from each foot.

Scientists argue about whether *Archaeopteryx* could fly. Unlike modern birds that fly, it had only a flat breastbone. Perhaps it ran and glided rather like a chicken does.

Insects were probably the main food of "ancient wing." Among its enemies were the flesh-eating dinosaurs such as *Compsognathus*.

Weight: Not known
Length: 3 feet (1 meter)
Found: Southern Germany
Lived: Late Jurassic

Archelon

This huge sea turtle belonged to one of the most ancient groups of reptiles – chelonians, ancestors of present-day tortoises and turtles. The first chelonians appeared about 210 million years ago. *Archelon* and its relatives lived during the Late Cretaceous Period in the seas of Europe and North America. In some ways *Archelon* resembled the living leathery turtle *Dermochelys*. It had a broad, flattened carapace (shell) and long paddle-shaped front limbs. Its head, however, was long and narrow, in contrast to the broad flat skull of *Dermochelys*. *Archelon*, like *Dermochelys*, lacked the numerous shell bones of tortoises. Horny plates covered its broad back.

Weight: Not known
Length: 10-13 feet (3-4 meters)
Found: North America
Lived: Late Cretaceous

Archelon

A

Arsinoitherium

Arsinoitherium

Scientists are rather baffled by this large twin-horned mammal. Remains of *Arsinoitherium* have been found in rocks in Egypt, in North Africa, dating from the Early Oligocene Epoch – 35-38 million years ago. They cannot trace its family history to a close ancestry with any particular group of living ungulates. No other animal has the same-shaped skeleton, although the shape and patterns of the cheek teeth are most similar to those of elephants, the rodent-like hyraxes, horses, and rhinos. *Arsinoitherium* looked like the modern rhinoceros, but it had a large head with two horns and heavy straight limbs like those of an elephant.

Weight: Not known
Length: 11 feet (3.4 meters)
Found: Egypt, North Africa
Lived: Early Oligocene

Australopithecus

Australopithecus is the name once widely used to describe the "southern ape men" of the Late Pliocene and Early Pleistocene Epochs. It is still used to refer to the heavily built *Australopithecus robustus* and the smaller *Australopithecus africanus*. But today many scientists agree that the first species is more distant from man and should be renamed *Paranthropus*, whereas the second is closer to man and should be renamed *Homo africanus*. A third species, *Australopithecus afarensis*, has been discovered, which is very close in form to the common ancestor of both *Paranthropus* and *Homo africanus*. All three lived in Africa 1.5-4 million years ago.

The head of the "southern ape man" had a mixture of humanlike and apelike features. The jaws projected like an ape's, and the brow ridges were prominent. But the teeth were more humanlike.

Paranthropus, *Homo africanus*, and *Australopithecus afarensis* may be regarded as mere ape men, but they stood and walked upright. They made crude tools and used animal bones as weapons. Some built shelters, and they hunted skillfully. Although their brain capacity was only one-third that of modern man, *Homo sapiens*, they were far more advanced than the first humanlike ape, *Ramapithecus*.

Australopithecus

Weight: Not known
Height: 4 feet (1.2 meters)
Found: Southern and Eastern Africa
Lived: Late Pliocene to Early Pleistocene

B

Baluchitherium

Baluchitherium

Weight: 17-18 tons (16 tonnes)
Length: 26 feet (8 meters)
Found: Asia
Lived: Oligocene to Miocene

Basilosaurus

Seagoing mammals appeared some 50 million years ago, during the Eocene Epoch. Whales, dugongs, and manatees were among the early ones. The first whales included the toothed *Basilosaurus*, or *Zeuglodon*. The form of their teeth suggests that their ancestors lived on land and that they were closely related to doglike animals, such as *Andrewsarchus*.

Ancestors of the rhinoceros appeared about 50 million years ago, during the Eocene Epoch. At first the rhinoceros family tree was dominated by small agile runners, such as *Hyrachyus*, with slim legs and long-toed feet. Like camels and goats, rhinos are ungulates – hoofed animals. But unlike the two-toed *Alticamelus*, rhinos always have at least three toes on the fore and hind feet.

Baluchitherium, or *Paraceratherium*, was a very large true rhinoceros that lived in Asia. In contrast to other rhinos, it was hornless. Its long legs, which were like columns, supported a heavy body. Adult animals stood 18 feet (5.5 meters) tall and weighed about 17-18 tons – one of the largest land animals ever known. *Baluchitherium* fed on leafy twigs that it plucked from the higher branches of trees.

Basilosaurus had a streamlined shape, with a sharp snout, two paddlelike front limbs, and a horizontal tail. The tail helped propel its serpentlike body through the water, and the limbs were used for steering. Fish was the main food of *Basilosaurus*, but smaller seagoing mammals could easily fall prey to its saw-edged teeth. At 66 feet (20 meters) in length, *Basilosaurus* was the giant in its day. Toothed whales appeared about 40 million years ago in the area of North America. Baleen, or filter-feeding, whales appeared earlier – some 45 million years ago – in India.

Weight: Not known
Length: 66 feet (20 meters)
Found: Africa, North America
Lived: Eocene to Early Oligocene

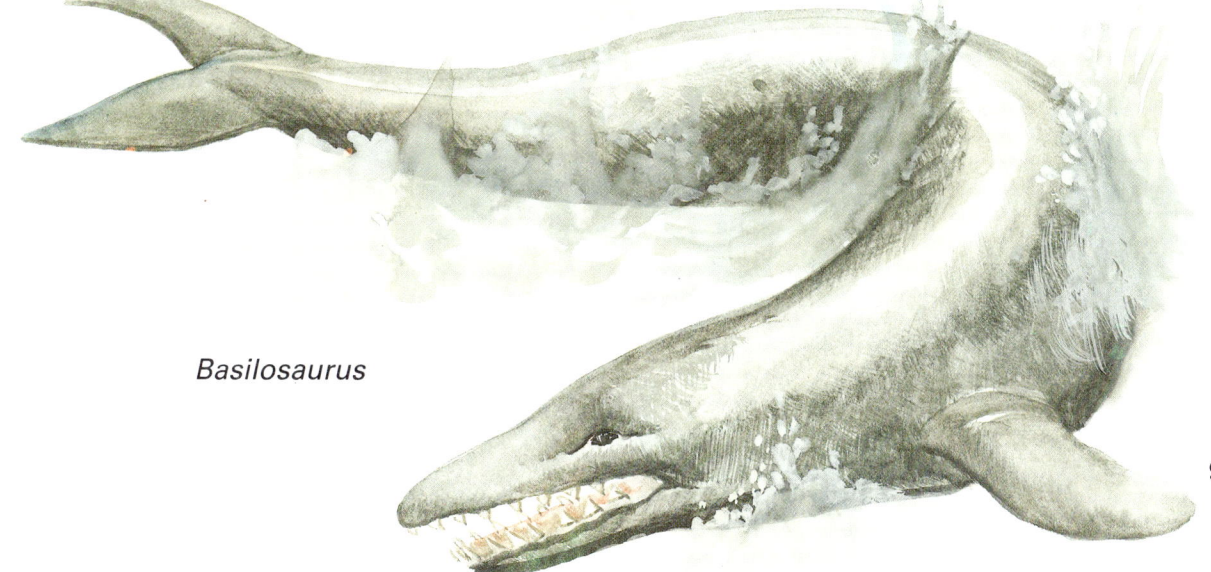
Basilosaurus

9

B

Brontotherium

During the Late Eocene and Early Oligocene Epochs, 30-45 million years ago, groups of large "odd-toed" ungulates (hoofed mammals) roamed the Earth. Odd-toed ungulates, or perissodactyls, tended to develop a strong central digit in the hand and foot, with two weaker digits to each side. In contrast, the "even-toed" ungulates, or artiodactyls, tended to develop two digits of equal strength.

Among the perissodactyls were brontotheres, huge animals with large bony knobs on their snouts. Their heavy limbs were like those of an elephant, but overall, they looked more like a rhino.

Brontotherium had a Y-shaped horn on its snout. It had four hoofed toes on each front foot and three on each hind foot. It ate soft leaves or grass, grinding its food with large flat cheek teeth.

Weight: Not known
Length: 16 feet (5 meters)
Found: North America
Lived: Oligocene

Brontotherium

Cheirolepis

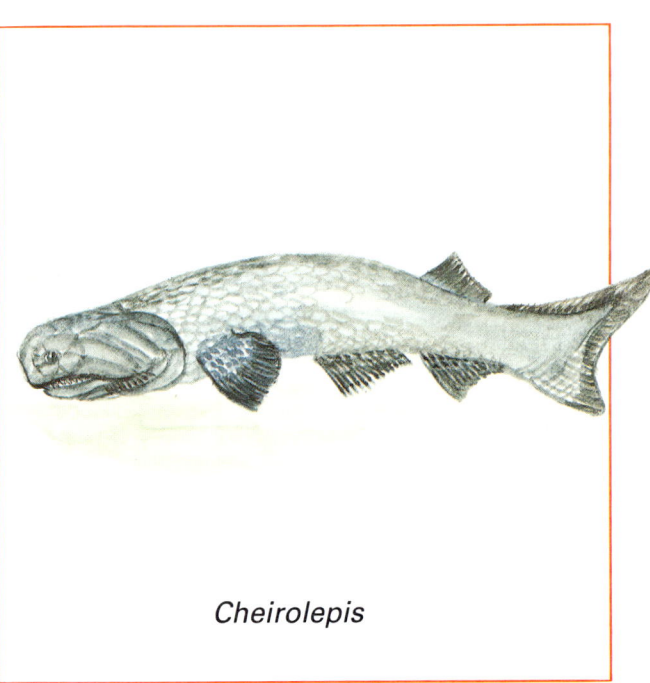
Cheirolepis

Fishes such as the shark and its relatives, with skeletons made of a gristly cartilage, have a very ancient ancestry. Fishes with bony skeletons, such as salmon and pike, have more recent origins. The first bony fishes appeared about 390 million years ago, during the Devonian Period. Among bony fishes, the lungfishes and their relatives have rounded fleshy fins, whereas the salmon and the pike have fan-shaped fins composed of many bony rays.

Cheirolepis was an early ray-finned fish that lived during the Middle Devonian. It was covered with heavy scales and had an uptilted, rather stubby tail. Bony plates covered the skull, and the eyes were located down low and toward the front of the head. *Cheirolepis* had only one fin on its back, unlike the lungfish, which has two. *Cheirolepis* resembled a herring, and we can assume that it was one of the ancestors of the fishes that now populate our rivers, lakes, and seas.

Weight: Not known
Length: Not known
Found: Europe, North America
Lived: Devonian

C

Coelodonta

During the last Ice Age, ice covered almost one-third of the Earth's surface, including large areas of Europe, Asia, and North America. Intense cold forced animals to move southward or to adapt to the conditions. Among those that were able to survive was the Woolly Rhinoceros. The scientific name given to this large plant-eater is *Coelodonta*. Skeletons, and cave paintings produced by early humans, provide us with exact details of its shape and shaggy appearance. The head was long, with a large horn above the nostrils and a smaller one between the eyes. For such a large animal, *Coelodonta* had rather small ears. They were almost hidden in the thick hair that crowned its head and covered its shoulders.

Coelodonta

Weight: Not known
Length: Not known
Found: Europe, Asia
Lived: Pleistocene

Cryptoclidus

Some reptiles returned to the sea during the Triassic Period. The plesiosaurs and pliosaurs were among the marine reptiles of the Mesozoic Era. The plesiosaurs had long necks, the pliosaurs short necks.

Cryptoclidus was a member of the long-necked group. It was a fast, agile swimmer that used its paddles in a manner similar to that of large sea turtles. The leatherback turtle *Dermochelys* moves the front paddles through a low figure eight, a kind of underwater flight that pushes the animal through the water. *Cryptoclidus* may have moved both front and back limbs through the same movements. Plesiosaurs fed on the fishes and shellfish that swam in the surface waters of the Jurassic and Cretaceous seas. The short-necked pliosaurs lived in the same seas with *Cryptoclidus*.

Weight: Not known
Length: 15 feet (4.6 meters)
Found: Europe
Lived: Late Jurassic

Cryptoclidus

C

Cynognathus

Cynognathus

Warm-blooded mammals appeared during the Triassic Period, which began 225 million years ago. Before their appearance, reptiles with mammal-like teeth and bones were present throughout the world. These reptiles were probably warm-blooded and gave birth to live young. Among these mammal-like reptiles was a group of small- to medium-sized meat eaters.

This group included *Cynognathus*, a reptile with a doglike skull. *Cynognathus* was the size of a wolf. It could run quite quickly when hunting its prey. Many of the skull features of *Cynognathus* were partly like those of mammals. Unlike the teeth in other reptiles, the teeth of advanced mammal-like reptiles resembled those of mammals and were separated into incisors, canines, and cheek teeth. The incisors were used for cutting, the canines for gripping and tearing, and the ridged cheek teeth for chewing.

Weight: Not known
Length: 5 feet (1.5 meters)
Found: Africa
Lived: Early to Middle Triassic

Deinotherium

Modern Indian and African elephants are the surviving members of a group that was once more numerous, varied, and widespread. The group is known as the Proboscidea, or long-snouted mammals. They first appeared during the Early Oligocene Epoch, when they were represented by such pig-sized trunkless animals as *Phiomia*. By the Miocene three distinct groups of proboscideans had appeared, including the deinotheres. Of these the best known is *Deinotherium*, a medium-sized beast with tusks in the lower jaw.

Deinotherium and its relatives are known as the hoe-tuskers. Their down-curved tusks may have been used for digging up roots. The trunk of *Deinotherium* was long and muscular, and worked effectively like a hand when the animal dug and pulled at roots and branches. Known from Africa and Asia, *Deinotherium* lived during the Miocene, Pliocene, and Pleistocene Epochs, a span of some 27.5 million years. It was once thought that *Deinotherium* and the other hoe-tuskers were river dwellers that used their tusks to anchor themselves to the riverbank while they slept.

Weight: Not known
Height: 13 feet (4 meters)
Found: Africa, Asia
Lived: Miocene to Pleistocene

Deinotherium

D

Deltatheridium

Deltatheridium

At the close of the Cretaceous Period, some 70 million years ago, most mammals were small insectivores, or insect eaters. *Deltatheridium* was one of the largest insect eaters at that time, and it may also have scavenged previously killed carcasses. Its cheek teeth had broad triangular crowns, which some scientists believe resembled those of marsupials, or pouched mammals. *Deltatheridium* looked most closely like a small weasel. Its ancestry lies very near the split of the two great groups of living mammals – the marsupials and the placentals, whose babies develop inside a maternal sac during pregnancy.

Weight: Not known
Length: 6 inches (15 centimeters)
Found: Mongolia
Lived: Late Cretaceous

Desmostylus

Scientists group elephants and sea cows together because their teeth show similarities – they both have teeth that move forward in their jaws as they become worn from chewing. This group, called the subungulates, includes hoofless mammals, both land-dwelling and sea-dwelling, that are closely related to ungulates.

Desmostylus, which belongs to this group, was a sea dweller that resembled the modern walrus. It and its relatives spread along the coasts of the northern Pacific Ocean during the Miocene and Early Pliocene Epochs. Its streamlined body and powerful paddlelike limbs made this animal well adapted to a life in the water.

Short tusks projected forward from the upper and lower jaws of *Desmostylus*. They were probably used for dislodging shellfish from the seafloor. Once loosened, the shells would be taken into the mouth and crushed between the closely packed heavily enameled cheek teeth.

Weight: Not known
Length: Not known
Found: Northern Pacific coasts
Lived: Miocene to Early Pliocene

Desmostylus

D

Dicrocerus

Dicrocerus, the first of the true deer, looked like a small roe deer. It lived in the Miocene and Pliocene Epochs, 7-26 million years ago. It had two small branched antlers on the top of its head. As with the modern deer, *Dicrocerus* rarely used its antlers in battle, although the males would lock in combat to defend their territory during the mating season.

Deer evolved from the same line as cattle, and deer and giraffes also probably share a common ancestor. Large numbers and many types of deer appeared by the dawn of the Pliocene Epoch.

Dicrocerus

Weight: Not known
Length: Not known
Found: Europe, Asia
Lived: Miocene to Pliocene

Dimetrodon

When full grown, *Dimetrodon* reached 11½ feet (3.5 meters) in length. Its sizable head had powerful jaws set with many sharp teeth for eating flesh.

The large sail of skin over the back of the *Dimetrodon* made its body appear very large. The sail was supported by vertical bony spines. It may have served to control the animal's body temperature, giving it an advantage over the animals on which it fed. When *Dimetrodon* stirred in the morning, it would turn so that the sail faced the sun. The heat absorbed quickly warmed the animal's blood, and the large flesh-eater would soon be ready to hunt and kill.

Dimetrodon and its relatives showed several mammal-like characteristics and were among the more distant ancestors of the warm-blooded mammals. Unlike the mammals or even the dinosaurs, however, *Dimetrodon* walked with a sprawling gait, directing its legs outward and then downward.

Weight: 550 pounds (250 kilograms)
Length: 11 feet 6 inches (3.5 meters)
Found: North America
Lived: Middle Permian

Dimetrodon

D

Dimorphodon

Dimorphodon

Dimorphodon was a flying reptile, or pterosaur. Pterosaurs appeared toward the end of the Triassic Period, some 225 million years ago. The oldest pterosaurs are known from Italy. *Dimorphodon* was somewhat younger, dating from the Lower Jurassic Period of southern England.

Compared with some of its descendants, *Dimorphodon* was of modest size, with a wingspan of only 5 feet (1.5 meters). It was, however, larger than some other true fliers, such as *Rhamphorynchus* and the hairy *Sordes pilosus*.

The wing of *Dimorphodon* was formed of skin stretched between the long inner finger of the hand and the thigh. Three clawed fingers on the front of the wing helped the animal to climb and to hold on when it was roosting. The tail was long with a flattened diamond-shaped tip. The head was large, with many sharp teeth in each jaw. Insects were the usual food of small pterosaurs, with several of the larger ones adapted to catching and eating fish.

Weight: Not known
Wingspan: 5 feet (1.5 meters)
Found: Southern England
Lived: Early Jurassic

Diplocaulus

Amphibians appeared during the Devonian Period, about 350 million years ago. They were the first animals with backbones to walk on land. Like modern frogs and toads, the earliest amphibians needed to live close to water so that they could lay their eggs, or spawn, there. Unlike reptile eggs, amphibian eggs have no shell, and unless they are laid in water, they will dry up.

The first amphibians ate fish and insects. Some were heavy creatures covered with scales. *Diplocaulus* appeared during the Late Carboniferous to Early Permian Period, some 270 million years ago. Compared with the large heavy-limbed amphibians that existed during the Devonian and Carboniferous Periods, *Diplocaulus* was of medium size with weak limbs. The animal had a broad head that most closely resembled a boomerang.

Weight: Not known
Length: 3 feet (1 meter)
Found: North America
Lived: Late Carboniferous to Permian

Diplocaulus

D

Diplovertebron

During the Carboniferous Period (280-345 million years ago) large areas of Europe and North America were covered by swamps and deltas. The warm, humid climate in these places was ideal for amphibians, and many new types appeared. Among these was *Diplovertebron*, a small amphibian whose teeth had a complicated folded structure. It was among several fossil amphibians that were closely related to reptiles.

Weight: Not known
Length: Not known
Found: Europe, North America
Lived: Late Carboniferous

Diplovertebron

Diprotodon

Diprotodon

Marsupials are animals with pouches. When their young are born, the babies are tiny and undeveloped. They crawl up into the pouch where they grow until they can fend for themselves. Marsupials are most widespread in Australia. They have developed there without competition from placental mammals, whose babies develop inside the maternal sac. Flesh-eating and plant-eating marsupials have evolved that closely resemble the placental dogs, cats, and deer.

During the past 50 million years, many marsupials grew to the size of a lion or a rhinoceros. *Diprotodon* was a huge marsupial that has been compared to the living hippo and rhino. It is actually a close relative of the living wombat, another marsupial. At 11 feet (3.4 meters) long, *Diprotodon* was obviously too large to burrow, as the wombat does. This animal probably lived near the edges of lakes, but it probably spent little time below water.

Weight: Not known
Length: 11 feet (3.4 meters)
Found: Australia
Lived: Pleistocene

Dipterus

This lungfish lived during Middle Devonian Period. It had a long body with paired leaf-shaped pectoral fins. The body and head were covered with scales much thicker than those found on living lungfishes. *Dipterus* had two fins down the center of its upper rear body, just in front of an uptilted tail.

Modern lungfishes live in ponds and lakes that evaporate in the dry season. Some can survive in shallow stagnant pools, while others survive by burrowing into the bottom mud. They continue to live in these burrows until the rainy season refills the ponds and lakes.

Weight: 3.25-3.5 pounds (1.5 kilograms)
Length: 1 foot 2 inches (36 centimeters)
Found: Europe, North America
Lived: Middle Devonian

D

Drepanaspis

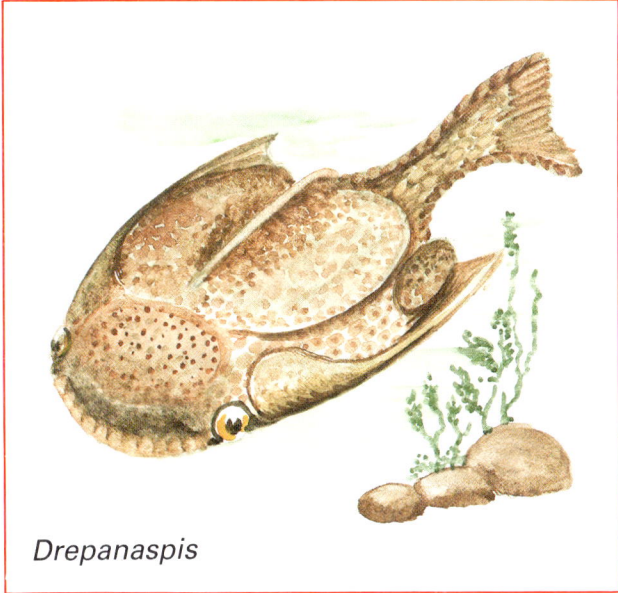
Drepanaspis

Dunkleosteus

"Plated-skin" fishes were abundant in the Devonian Period. They are unique with their distinct head and chest shields. The scientific name *placoderm* aptly describes the thick heavy armor covering the end of the body, which protected the animals against their enemies. Placoderms may have been closely related to modern sharks.

Dunkleosteus was the giant of the group. It grew to over 30 feet (9 meters) in length. Its armored head and jointed neck regions measured 10 feet (3 meters) long. This monster had large toothlike plates on the margins of the upper and lower jaws, which it used to cut into its prey. Behind the head, the body tapered to a point, with long fin structures stretching from about halfway along the body to the tip of the tail, on both upper and lower surfaces.

Dunkleosteus

Although the first fishes appeared during the Early Ordovician Period, nearly 500 million years ago, it was not until the Devonian that they became common in both fresh and salt water. The Devonian *Drepanaspis* was a flattened bottom-dweller whose head and gills formed a distinctive spadelike shape. It had small eyes located on the front outside edge of the head. A number of large plates formed part of the body armor. Smaller five-sided plates ringed the central areas of both upper and lower surfaces. It was a poor swimmer, with a rather stubby, sideways flattened tail. Unlike many modern free-swimming bony fishes, such as trout, *Drepanaspis* sucked up its food from the seabed.

Weight: 2.25 pounds (1 kilogram)
Length: 1 foot (30 centimeters)
Found: Europe
Lived: Early Devonian

Dunkleosteus lived near the seabed and darted forward and upward with a wiggly motion to kill its prey.

Weight: Not known
Length: 30 feet (9 meters)
Found: North America, Europe
Lived: Late Devonian

Dipterus

E

Edaphosaurus

Like *Dimetrodon*, *Edaphosaurus* belonged to the group Pelycosauria, sail-backed mammal-like reptiles from the Early Permian Period. Long vertical spines with distinctive crossbars supported its sail of skin. The sail looked something like the ribbed shell of an oyster, with rear spines curving backward toward the tail. As with *Dimetrodon*, the sail probably helped the animal to control its body temperature.

Neither *Edaphosaurus* nor *Dimetrodon* was a direct ancestor of mammals. Both were low, squat animals that walked on all fours. They were sprawlers that waggled lizardlike over the stony ground of the Permian world. Short-headed, large-eyed *Edaphosaurus* lived on the edges of lakes and swamps where plants flourished in an otherwise barren world.

In contrast with *Dimetrodon*, a fierce flesh-eater, *Edaphosaurus* was a gentle vegetarian. It fed on rough plants, crushing them to pulp with blunt teeth in its jaws and on the roof of its mouth.

Weight: 660 pounds (300 kilograms)
Length: 11 feet (3.3 meters)
Found: Europe, North America
Lived: Late Permian

Elasmotherium

Rhinoceroses and their trunk-snouted relatives the tapirs appeared some 50 million years ago. At first they were small animals that lived in forest glades and clearings. Over time, however, rhinoceroses developed heavy bodies and thick, hoofed limbs.

Elasmotherium was a browser that fed on leaves and grasses on the northern plains of Europe and Asia. It grew to the size of an elephant, almost twice the length of today's rhino. Like the present-day Indian rhino, it had a single horn at the front of its snout. But the horn of *Elasmotherium* was a huge 6½ feet (2 meters) long.

In most reconstructions, scientists portray *Elasmotherium* with a thick furry coat. This would have helped it survive the cold of the northern lands during the great Ice Age. The coat, however, was shorter than that of the Woolly Rhinoceros, which probably lived closer to the edge of the glacier advance. Rhinoceroses relied on bulk rather than on speed for protection. We know that an enraged rhino is a fearsome sight, and the animal is capable of inflicting serious injury on a threatening foe.

Edaphosaurus

E

Elasmotherium

Weight: 3.5-4.5 tons (3-4 tonnes)
Length: 26 feet (8 meters)
Found: Europe, Asia
Lived: Pleistocene

Eryops

At the same time that the sail-backed reptiles, such as *Dimetrodon* and *Edaphosaurus*, ruled the world, large amphibians such as *Eryops* lived in swamps. Compared with living frogs and toads, *Eryops* was enormous. It had a heavy body with a strong backbone and a broad skull with many sharp teeth. Because of the folded pattern of the enamel that covered the teeth, *Eryops* is termed a labyrinthodont amphibian. It might be aptly described as a kind of amphibian crocodile.

On land *Eryops* moved on short, strong limbs. Although it was a flesh eater, it would have been easy prey for the much larger, more agile *Dimetrodon*. So it spent much time in the water, swimming with the aid of its strong tail and feeding on lobe-finned fishes.

A close relative of *Eryops*, called *Cacops*, also lived in the waters of the Permian swamps. *Cacops* had a much larger head, and its back was protected by bony plates.

Weight: Not known
Length: 5 feet (1.5 meters)
Found: North America
Lived: Permian

Eryops

E

Eunotosaurus

This small reptile from the Permian Period of South Africa is unique. *Eunotosaurus* had long been considered to be closely related to turtles because of its broad ribs, which were so expanded that they nearly touched one another. The shell, or carapace, of turtles, however, is not formed by the ribs. It is formed by bony plates that fuse to ribs of normal proportions. *Eunotosaurus*, therefore, is not closely related to turtles. Its true ancestry remains a puzzling question.

Weight: Not known
Length: 6 inches (15 centimeters)
Found: South Africa
Lived: Permian

Eunotosaurus

Eusthenopteron

Eusthenopteron

Lobe-finned fishes were common during the Devonian Period. They included lungfishes such as *Dipterus* and the carnivorous freshwater fish *Eusthenopteron*. The latter was an active hunter that lurked in shallow waters. As with other lobe-finned fishes, there were several bones in the paired fins that resembled the bones in the limbs of land animals. A distinct long bone in the forelimb, the humerus, had developed, and the animal may have used the strengthened fin for support or for navigating through shallow water thick with vegetation. The fins of *Eusthenopteron* represent a stage in the evolution toward the walking limbs that were first found in amphibians. The form of the skull and backbone in this animal also suggests a close link with the first land dwellers.

Weight: Not known
Length: 1-2 feet (30-60 centimeters)
Found: Europe, North America
Lived: Devonian

G

Gerrothorax

The Triassic landscape was marked by the presence of rugged mountains, sand dunes, and lowland lakes. Reptiles were the dominant land animals, but within lake waters small to medium-size amphibians were common. Among these was the strange larval-like *Gerrothorax*. It looked like a large tadpole that had failed to change into an adult frog. Its head was short and wide, with two eyes close together at the front, behind two small nostrils. Just in front of the two rather weak four-fingered front limbs were external gills for breathing in water. The tail was small, and the back legs were also small and prabably webbed at the fingers.

Gerrothorax is thought to have lived at the water's edge, gulping at water insects or small fishes. It would rarely, if ever, have left the water, and it is difficult to imagine that this animal was a strong swimmer.

Glyptodon

Gerrothorax

Glyptodon

Often described as a mammal tortoise, *Glyptodon* was a large heavily armored plant eater. It is a relative of the modern armadillo. But instead of armor arranged in bands around the body, the armor of this ancient South American giant was fused into a solid structure similar to a turtle shell. The shell was dome shaped and covered the upper body from behind the head to the beginning of the tail. A bony cap covered the head, and the tail was protected by many bony rings.

Glyptodon had short heavy limbs. The front feet had five clawed toes, and the back feet were shaped like hooves. The head and jaws were very tall, and the snout was short. *Glyptodon* probably spent most of its life searching for food and munching. Later in the Pleistocene relatives of *Glyptodon* migrated toward the northwest, into North America, across a land bridge.

Weight: Not known
Length: 3 feet (1 meter)
Found: Europe
Lived: Late Triassic

Weight: Not known
Length: 10 feet (3 meters)
Found: South America
Lived: Pliocene to Pleistocene

G

Gomphotherium

Gomphotherium

This Miocene four-tusker was closely related to *Phiomia*, an Early Oligocene proboscidean, or long-snouted mammal. In fact, *Gomphotherium*, like its ancestor, had a relatively short trunk. The lower jaw was long with two short broad tusks at the end. The upper tusks were straighter, rounded, and directed outward, away from the sides of the trunk. It is possible that *Gomphotherium* dug for roots, but perhaps not as efficiently as the hoe-tusker *Deinotherium*. The tusks and short trunk may have been used to break up branches or gather food. Another new relative of *Gomphotherium* was the "shovel-tusker" *Platybelodon*.

Weight: 2.75 tons (2.5 tonnes)
Length: 19 feet (6 meters)
Found: Europe, Asia, Africa, North America
Lived: Miocene

Hemicyclaspis

Hemicyclaspis was a jawless fish from the Late Silurian to Early Devonian Periods. Its suckerlike mouth was located on the underside of its head. On the topside, two eyes were set close together, high on the face. The head was protected by a solid bony shield and the body by numerous plates that allowed it to flex from side to side. Two "horns" swept back from the rear edges of the skull. The body was triangular in cross section, and the tail uptilted toward its tip.

It is likely that *Hemicyclaspis* was a bottom dweller, and that it sucked its food from the soft mud. Touch-sensitive areas on the sides of the headshield helped *Hemicyclaspis* guide itself past rocks and pebbles. Like *Drepanaspis*, *Hemicyclaspis* had an internal skeleton composed of cartilage rather than of bone. These fishes lived mainly in rivers and freshwater lakes.

Hemicyclaspis

Weight: Not known
Length: 5 inches (13 centimeters)
Found: Europe, North America
Lived: Late Silurian to Early Devonian

H

Hesperornis

The skeletons of birds are light and rather delicate. The bones are hollow but strong enough to support the powerful muscles needed for flight. Their delicate nature, however, means that they are not easily fossilized, and the number of birds recorded in the fossil record is rather limited. This is particularly true before the Eocene, and rare finds, such as *Hesperornis*, are of very great importance.

Hesperornis – "western bird" – was a diver. It had a long, toothed beak and powerful hind limbs with webbed feet. The wings were too small to support flight. On land *Hesperornis* was rather awkward, but in the water it was a powerful swimmer. It probably lived close to the water on rocky coasts, where it could feed on fish. On land other ancient birds, such as *Ichthyornis*, were strong fliers, like the many kinds of songbirds we see today.

Weight: Not known
Length: 3 feet (1 meter)
Found: North America
Lived: Late Cretaceous

Hesperornis

Hipparion

Hipparion

The evolution of the horse began some 55 million years ago. The first horse was the small, dog-sized ungulate *Hyracotherium*. By the Pliocene Epoch, horses looked similar to the modern horse.

Hipparion belonged to a different evolutionary line from that of the modern horse, *Equus*. It was about the size of a pony. It was lightly built, and its strong legs could carry it at a fast gallop. Whereas the modern horse has a single hoofed toe, *Hipparion* had three-toed feet.

Hipparion first appeared in North America and spread across the Bering land bridge to Asia and then to Europe. It lived on the open plains and grasslands of the northern continents. *Hipparion* survived for about 5 million years, into the Early Pleistocene.

Weight: Not known
Length: 7 feet (2.2 meters)
Found: Europe, Asia, North America
Lived: Late Miocene to Early Pleistocene

H

Homo erectus

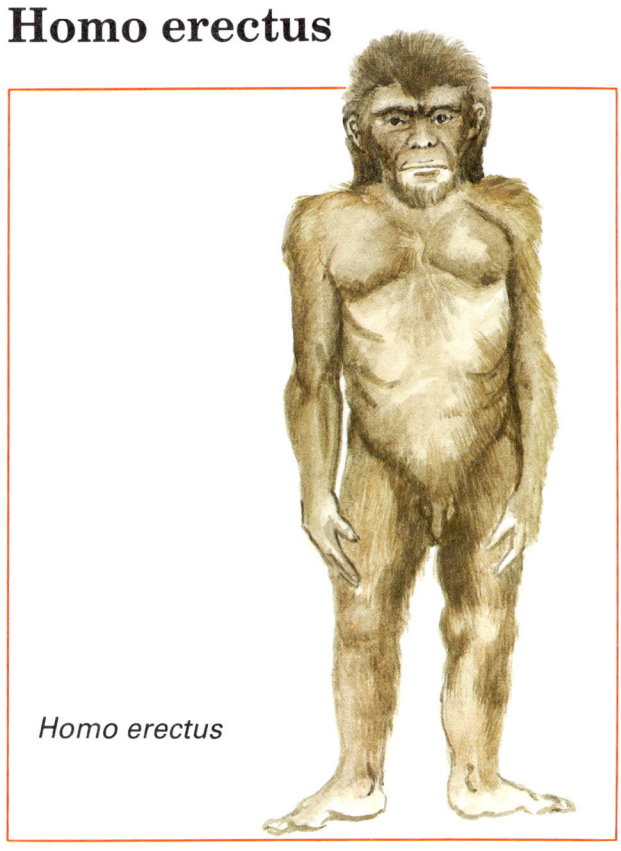

Homo erectus

Weight: 126 pounds (57 kilograms)
Height: 5 feet 6 inches (1.7 meters)
Found: Africa, Europe, Asia
Lived: Pliocene to Pleistocene

The first appearance of fossils along the lineage leading to *Homo sapiens* – modern man – began 4 million years ago, during the Pliocene. *Homo afarensis* was the first of the line, followed by *Homo africanus* and then *Homo habilis* ("handyman") and *Homo erectus* ("upright man"). Each of these showed important changes pointing toward modern man, as well as other characteristics that were peculiar to each species.

Homo erectus was quite tall and walked upright. These creatures looked similar to us, but they had heavy ridges over the eyes and larger teeth and jaws than we have. The forehead sloped back slightly and the brain had about three-quarters of the capacity of *Homo sapiens* – you and me.

Homo erectus used tools and weapons and was the first of the human line to use fire. The construction of shelters and the wearing of skins enabled *Homo erectus* to travel northward from Africa into Europe and Asia. *Homo erectus* hunted deer, elephant, and rhinoceros. Evidence also exists to suggest that they were cannibals.

Hylonomus

Among the differences between amphibians and reptiles are the different sorts of eggs they lay. Amphibians lay their eggs in water or in damp areas. The eggs are often protected by a jelly to keep them from drying out. Reptile eggs do not share this problem because they are enclosed in a shell.

Although a reptile is an animal that lays shelled eggs, eggs are rarely found far back in the fossil record. We must also look at the skeleton to identify the earliest reptiles. *Hylonomus*, one of the first reptiles, is recorded from the Carboniferous sediments of Nova Scotia, in Canada. It was a small animal with a relatively deep skull, a short neck, and a long tail. The spine was strong, and the limbs spread outward and downward, resulting in a sprawling gait. The remains of *Hylonomus* are found in fossil treetrunks in which the animals became trapped. *Hylonomus* was the ancient forerunner of turtles, lizards, crocodiles, and birds.

Weight: Not known
Length: 8-12 inches (20-30 centimeters)
Found: Canada
Lived: Late Carboniferous

Hylonomus

H

Hyracodon

The early rhinoceroses were agile running animals. *Hyracodon*, which appeared during the Oligocene, was one of the very first rhinoceroses. It was small, and its head was more like that of a donkey than that of a rhinoceros. The legs were slim, and the feet had three long toes. *Hyracodon* was very different in appearance from the heavy, hippolike rhinoceroses, such as *Baluchitherium*. It was a plant eater, and the shape of the teeth indicate that it was a browser, feeding on leaves.

Hyracodon

Weight: Not known
Length: 5 feet (1.5 meters)
Found: North America
Lived: Oligocene

Hyracotherium

Hyracotherium

Also known as *Eohippus*, *Hyracotherium* was the first horse. It lived in Europe and North America, in forest glades or clearings, where it browsed on leaves. *Hyracotherium* was the size of a medium-sized dog or fox. Compared with modern horses, it had a short neck and a short snout. The wrinkles on the crowns of the teeth were simpler than those of modern horses, which have more ridges for grinding food.

Hyracotherium had slim legs with four-toed front feet and three-toed back feet. It was an agile animal that could dart quickly to avoid trouble. Modern horses have strong single-hoofed legs. They can run quickly, and they live as grazers on open plains. The horses between *Hyracotherium* and *Equus* show a steady succession of changes that lead to the modern form.

Weight: Not known
Length: 1 foot 8 inches (50 centimeters)
Found: Europe, North America
Lived: Eocene

I

Ichthyornis

Ichthyornis

Of the earliest birds, *Archaeopteryx, Hesperornis,* and *Ichthyornis* are the best known. All three had teeth, but only *Ichthyornis*, the "fish bird," was certainly a powerful flier. It was small and stout, like a tern. Its head was rounded; its long slim beak full of small curved teeth. Unlike *Archaeopteryx*, it had a well-developed keeled breastbone to support powerful flight muscles.

Ichthyornis was a fish eater. It lived on shorelines and flew over the sea in search of food. Like modern-day gulls and terns, the "fish bird" lived in flocks. Nesting sites were probably along the shores and cliffs. Other birds, small reptiles, and small rodentlike mammals may have been its nest robbers.

Weight: Not known
Length: 8 inches (20 centimeters)
Found: North America
Lived: Late Cretaceous

Ichthyosaurus

This name was once used to describe several types of fish-eating lizards that lived during the Middle to Late Jurassic Period. It is now used for a single animal within the group. When "fish lizards" appeared during the Triassic, *Mixosaurus* was one of the first. It had a long tail with ribbonlike fins above and below.

The largest *Ichthyosaurus* grew to 25 feet (7.5 meters) in length. *Ichthyosaurus* had a large tail similar to that of a shark. It also had a beautifully streamlined body and a large dorsal fin. These features suggest that the animal resembled a shark or a dolphin quite closely. *Ichthyosaurus* and its relatives were excellent swimmers. They had small paddlelike limbs, suitable only for steering. The body and tail provided most of the propulsion. *Ichthyosaurus* was unable to leave the water to lay eggs. Female animals with the young still inside the body show that the "fish lizards" overcame this problem by giving birth to live young.

Weight: Not known
Length: Up to 25 feet (7.5 meters)
Found: Worldwide
Lived: Middle to Late Jurassic

Ichthyosaurus

Ichthyostega

Amphibians evolved from the "lobe-finned" fishes during the Devonian Period. *Ichthyostega* was one of the first amphibians. Because its teeth were folded into a complicated structure – similar to that of *Eryops* – it is grouped among the labyrinthodonts.

Ichthyostega

The skull of *Ichthyostega* showed several important changes from that of the fish, one being a smaller total number of bones. Also, it had better developed ears and more efficient lungs. *Ichthyostega* had a fishlike tail. But in contrast to fishes such as *Eusthenopteron*, which had rounded fleshy fins, it had strong limbs. They were directed outward and downward, supporting the weight of the animal's body and giving it a sprawling side-to-side walk.

Amphibians' conquest of the harsh conditions on land was only a partial success. They still had to keep their skin moist and needed to return to the water to lay their eggs.

Weight: Not known
Length: 3 feet (1 meter)
Found: Greenland
Lived: Late Devonian

Indricotherium

Like *Baluchitherium (Paraceratherium)*, *Indricotherium* was a giant hornless rhino. It lived in Asia, where it roamed over shrub-covered lands and browsed on plants. It had a large head, a huge body, and massive limbs. *Indricotherium* was smaller than *Baluchitherium* – and was probably the larger animal's ancestor. It survived throughout the Oligocene Epoch, a period of about 14 million years, 26-40 million years ago. Among the natural enemies of this great beast were the flesh-eating *Hyaenodon* and *Dinictis*.

Indricotherium

Weight: 10 tons (9 tonnes)
Length: 16 feet (5 meters)
Found: Asia
Lived: Oligocene

L

Lystrosaurus

During the Triassic Period reptiles and the first mammals conquered the land. Mammal-like reptiles ruled for the early part of the period but were replaced first by primitive archosaurs, resembling modern-day crocodiles – and then by the dinosaurs.

Among the mammal-like reptiles were the tusked dicynodonts. Their name simply means "two-dog-toothed." Instead of other teeth, they had a horny sheath. Dicynodonts fed on plants, chopping them into small pieces. Distant cousins, including *Cynognathus*, were flesh eaters.

Lystrosaurus

Lystrosaurus was one of the best-known dicynodonts. It was a small but heavy, bulky beast with a short stubby tail. Many skeletons of this animal have been found in South Africa, Asia, and Antarctica. These finds indicate that *Lystrosaurus* lived in herds and that the southern lands were at one time a single huge landmass. Scientists believe that *Lystrosaurus* stayed in and around the edges of lakes and swamps.

Weight: Not known
Length: 3 feet (1 meter)
Found: South Africa, Asia, Antarctica
Lived: Early Triassic

Machairodus

Machairodus

Saber-toothed cats had unusual upper canine teeth – very long and slightly curved. These teeth were used to stab and slice. *Machairodus* was a typical saber-tooth. It was strongly built. It had powerful muscles to snap its mouth closed and jaws that opened very wide. Together, the teeth, the muscles, and the powerful jaws indicate that animals such as *Machairodus* fed on thick-skinned beasts, including rhinoceroses and mammoths. They probably lay in wait and trapped old or sick animals after a short chase.

Saber-toothed cats were very successful animals and spread throughout the northern continents. Their success was linked with the spread of the thick-skinned plant eaters. *Machairodus* was one of the most successful of these large and unusual cats. During the Pleistocene, however, modern cats, such as the lion, the puma, and the leopard, appeared. Perhaps competition with these modern cats sealed the fate of the saber-toothed cats.

Weight: 165 pounds (75 kilograms)
Length: 5 feet (1.5 meters)
Found: Northern continents
Lived: Pliocene to Early Pleistocene

M

Macrauchenia

This odd-looking animal lived on the South American landmass during the Pleistocene. *Macrauchenia* was a hoofed animal with a long neck and a muscular body. It looked like a camel. It browsed on leaves and twigs from high tree branches.

Macrauchenia belonged to a group of animals that lived only in South America at a time when the two Americas were separated by a sea across the region of Central America. This group, known as litopterns, developed without competition from the more advanced northern mammals, such as true camels, llamas, and giraffes. They were not preyed upon by the large fierce cats and dogs that lived in the north. Without these animals, the South American groups evolved forms comparable to camels, horses, and rodents. When North and South America were reconnected by a land bridge during the Pleistocene, the northern mammals swarmed south and the litopterns and many other groups died out.

Weight: Not known
Length: 10 feet (3 meters)
Found: South America
Lived: Pleistocene

Macrauchenia

Mammuthus

Mammuthus is the scientific name for mammoths. These great beasts first appeared at the end of the Pliocene Epoch, some 2 million years ago, probably in Africa. They are closely related to modern elephants, particularly the Indian elephant, and to the curved-tusked *Stegodon* that lived in Asia and Africa. During the Ice Age, mammoths survived quite successfully, and they were found throughout Europe until 9,000 years ago.

Mammuthus

There was a wide range of mammoths, including dwarfed island forms such as *Elephas falconeri* and the huge straight-tusked forest dweller, *Palaeoloxodon*. This beast grew to 13 feet (4 meters) in height. The Imperial Mammoth, *Mammuthus imperator*, reached the same height and had tusks more than 13 feet (4 meters) long!

Weight: 3.25-3.5 tons (3 tonnes)
Length: 10-13 feet (3-4 meters)
Found: Worldwide
Lived: Pliocene to Early Holocene

M

Mammuthus primigenius

Mammuthus primigenius

This animal was the Woolly Mammoth. It grew to 9½ feet (2.9 meters) tall and had huge curved tusks. In contrast to *Stegodon*, from which it evolved, *Mammuthus primigenius* had a tall, broad skull. It had shorter jaws, and the cheek teeth had a more complex ridge-and-groove pattern on their upper surfaces. During the Ice Age the Woolly Mammoth lived in the northern parts of Europe, Asia, and North America, where great ice sheets covered the land. To protect itself from the cold, the beast had a very thick coat of reddish-brown hair. The huge tusks were used for defense as well as for digging into the snow in search of food.

Our knowledge of the Woolly Mammoth has been increased by the study of cave drawings made by early humans. The discovery of the mummified remains of several animals in the icy soil of Siberia has also helped. The mummies have their thick, hairy coats – as well as a thick layer of woolly underfur.

Weight: 3 tons (2.75 tonnes)
Length: 11 feet 6 inches (3.5 meters)
Found: Europe, Asia, North America
Lived: Pleistocene to Early Holocene

Mandasuchus

The ancestors of the dinosaurs appeared during the Late Permian Period, and we call the dinosaurs and their close relatives the "ruling reptiles," or archosaurs. Many of them were four-legged creatures, but some walked on only their hind legs.

Mandasuchus was a four-legged primitive archosaur. Like others of its kind, it resembled a modern crocodile or alligator. The primitive archosaur skull – like a dinosaur skull – had two holes behind the eyes. The backbone was strong and had about 24 vertebrae between the head and the hip. The back legs were longer than the front legs, and both front and back limbs were drawn close to the body. *Mandasuchus* was therefore more agile than many other reptiles of its era. It was a flesh eater, and it hunted mammal-like reptiles.

Weight: Not known
Length: 8 feet (2.5 meters)
Found: Africa
Lived: Middle Triassic

Mandasuchus

30

M

Mastodon

Many groups of elephants died out at the end of the Ice Age, leaving only the modern Indian and African elephants. *Mastodon* survived a little longer than other types. It lived in North America until 8,000 years ago. The mastodon family had appeared 35 million years earlier and had spread throughout Europe, Asia, North America, and North Africa.

Mastodon

Mastodon is known from numerous skeletons, many of which have been found in the swamps that covered parts of North America after the Ice Age. It was a forest browser and therefore lived farther away from the great ice sheets than the Woolly Mammoth. It had a large head with long upwardly curved tusks. The cheek teeth were strong with long crests across them. The adult animal grew more than 8 feet (2.5 meters) tall. Like the Woolly Mammoth, *Mastodon* had a coat of reddish-brown hair.

Weight: 1.7 tons (1.5 tonnes)
Length: 10 feet (3 meters)
Found: North America
Lived: Pleistocene to Holocene

Mastodonsaurus

Mastodonsaurus

Mastodonsaurus was the largest of the labyrinthodonts – amphibians with complexly folded, or labyrinthine, teeth. Its remains have been found in European rocks dating from the Triassic Period. It lived on the edges of swamps and lakes, along with the tadpolelike *Gerrothorax* and *Proganochelys*, the first turtle. *Mastodonsaurus* fed on fish. If it strayed too far from the safety of water, it in turn could provide an easy meal for a dinosaur or other reptile.

Mastodonsaurus was a "sprawler." Its strong legs pointed downward and outward, supporting a large, heavy body and a long tail. Its flat skull alone measured more than 3 feet (1 meter) in length.

Weight: Not known
Length: 10 feet 6 inches (3.2 meters)
Found: Europe, North Africa
Lived: Triassic

M

Megalichthys

During the Devonian and Carboniferous Periods, lobe-finned fishes were common in lakes and rivers. From our knowledge of *Eusthenopteron* we know that these fishes were probably ancestors of the amphibians. They were active flesh-eaters.

Megalichthys lived during the Carboniferous Period. It was 1-2 feet (30-60 centimeters) long and lived in freshwater ponds and streams. Like *Eusthenopteron*, it had a streamlined shape with a fairly broad slightly flat head. The tail was upturned.

Megalichthys fed on small animals such as insects and some amphibians. It had many sharp-pointed teeth and strong jaws. The body was long and slender and covered with small scales. Speed and agility were the keys to the success of *Megalichthys* and the other fast-swimming lobe-fins.

Weight: 3-4.5 pounds (1.5-2 kilograms)
Length: 1-2 feet (30-60 centimeters)
Found: Europe, North America
Lived: Carboniferous

Megalichthys

Weight: 3-4.5 pounds (1.5-2 kilograms)
Length: 1-2 feet (30-60 centimeters)
Found: Europe, North America
Lived: Carboniferous

Megaloceros

Giant animals roamed the Earth during the great Ice Age. These included the Woolly Mammoth, the Woolly Rhinoceros, and a giant beaver 9 feet (2.75 meters) long. Another huge animal was *Megaloceros giganteus*, the giant Irish elk. This deer stood over 10 feet (3 meters) tall, and had huge antlers. In large males the antlers were equal in width to the height of the animal. The name Irish elk is misleading because herds of these animals were not limited to Ireland but roamed Europe and Asia between 1.5 million and 2,500 years ago.

Megaloceros was a relative of the fallow deer. Modern deer have a four-chambered stomach that enables them to digest tough woody plant materials, and *Megaloceros* probably had the same. Like its living relatives, it shed its antlers each year. In North America the giant moose, *Cervacles*, occupied the same biological role as *Megaloceros*. The natural enemies of these animals were wolves and the large cats. Miniature versions of the Ice Age giants lived on small isolated islands in the Mediterranean.

Megaloceros

Weight: Not known
Length: 16 feet (5 meters)
Found: Europe, Asia
Lived: Pleistocene to Holocene

M

Megatherium

Megatherium was one of a mixed group of animals called the edentates. Modern edentates include the tree sloths, armadillos, and anteaters of South America; the aardvark of South Africa; and the strange scaly anteaters, or pangolins, of Africa and Asia. Edentates appeared some 60 million years ago in North America.

Megatherium, the largest ground sloth, evolved about 2 million years ago. It lived in both North and South America. At more than 20 feet (6 meters) long, heavily built *Megatherium* towered over other animals of its time. It was a plant eater. Walking slowly and ponderously on its knuckles, *Megatherium* was able to stretch up to feed on the top branches of trees. While feeding, the animal rested on its large strong tail.

The "hands" were clawed and the feet armed with two strong, pointed nails. *Megatherium* probably dug for roots as well as eating leaves and twigs. It had peglike teeth set in powerful jaws. In contrast to the gigantic forms of *Megatherium* that lived on the plains of America, cat-sized relatives lived on the islands of the Mediterranean Sea and the Indian Ocean.

Weight: 4.75 tons (4 tonnes)
Length: 20 feet (6 meters)
Found: North America, South America
Lived: Pliocene to Pleistocene

Megatherium

Megazostrodon

This tiny creature was one of the first mammals. *Megazostrodon* was only 4 inches (10 centimeters) long and a few ounces in weight. Its remains have been found in rocks from the Late Triassic to Early Jurassic Periods in southern Africa. A complete skeleton from Lesotho shows that this early mammal was more primitive in structure than any of the living mammals, including the duck-billed platypus and the spiny echidna. The earliest mammals were probably insect eaters feeding on beetles and flies. In Europe the first mammals were represented by *Morganucodon*, another mouse-sized form.

Weight: Not known
Length: 4 inches (10 centimeters)
Found: Southern Africa
Lived: Late Triassic to Early Jurassic

Megazostrodon

M

Merychippus

Horses appeared on Earth about 55 million years ago. They belong to the same group of mammals – perissodactyls, or odd-toed ungulates – as rhinoceroses and tapirs. Modern horses have hooves, but early ones had toes.

Merychippus was a pony-sized horse with three toes. Its middle toe formed a well-developed hoof, which helped it to run quickly across the grasslands of North America. It lived during the Miocene and Pliocene Epochs, from 26 to 7 million years ago. The adult animal stood a little over 3 feet (1 meter) tall. Its long neck and face were well suited for feeding on the grasses that covered the open plains.

The teeth of *Merychippus* were more complicated than those of its ancestors. A gap between the front teeth and the cheek teeth suggests that *Merychippus* could use its tongue to move food back to the cheek teeth for better grinding and chewing.

Mesohippus

Merychippus

Mesohippus

As horses evolved, new forms generally increased in size. Longer legs, a longer neck, and the gradual change from toes to hooves showed that the animals were becoming more suited to the open plains than to the forest glades. Strength and speed are assets that led to the survival of horses over the last 30 million years.

Mesohippus, which dates from the Oligocene Epoch, represents the halfway stage in the evolution of horses. In some ways it was more like a small deer than a horse. Adult animals of the *Mesohippus* stock grew only to about 3 feet (almost 1 meter) in height. It had a relatively short head and neck, as well as three-toed feet. Even in *Mesohippus* though, the middle toe showed some hooflike characteristics. This means that *Mesohippus* could probably trot and run just like a modern horse can. The presence of low-crowned simple teeth in *Mesohippus* suggests that this early horse still ate leaves rather than grass, which the modern horse eats.

Weight: Not known
Length: 6 feet 6 inches (2 meters)
Found: North America
Lived: Miocene to Pliocene

Weight: Not known
Length: 3 feet (1 meter)
Found: North America
Lived: Early to Middle Oligocene

M

Mesosaurus

Some reptiles returned to live in the water during the Carboniferous Period, about 300 million years ago. Among the first aquatic reptiles were the mesosaurs. A mesosaur was a slimly built creature with a long head and body and a thin tail. The tail was flattened sideways and was used in swimming. The animal also used its long back legs to push itself through the water. It may have used its smaller front limbs to help steer.

Mesosaurus had teeth on the roof of its mouth and around the edges of its jaws. The snout was slim, and the nostrils were placed well back near the eyes. The roof of the skull was solid and shows that *Mesosaurus* was related to the most primitive reptiles. But the exact ancestry of this strange animal remains unknown.

Mesosaurus

Mesosaurus probably hunted fish. The teeth on the roof of the mouth suggest that it may also have caught freshwater creatures such as shrimp and crayfish.

Weight: Not known
Length: 1 foot 6 inches (45 centimeters)
Found: South Africa, South America
Lived: Late Carboniferous to Early Permian

Metacheiromys

Unlike other edentates, such as *Megatherium* and *Glyptodon*, which were both giants, *Metacheiromys* was a small, doglike creature with a long low head, a long tail, and short legs. It had sharp canine teeth, and it probably used them to grasp the small animals on which it fed. Sharp claws suggest that *Metacheiromys* dug in search of its prey. It lived about 50 million years ago and is thought to have been the ancestor of anteaters and sloths.

Weight: Not known
Length: 1 foot 6 inches (45 centimeters)
Found: North America
Lived: Middle Eocene

Metacheiromys

M

Metamynodon

Scientists believe that *Metamynodon* was a distant relative of the modern rhinoceros. *Metamynodon* was a water-loving creature that lived in lakes and rivers, probably in family groups. It looked much more like a hippopotamus than like a rhino. It lived some 30 million years ago during the Oligocene. The last relative of this strange hornless stock died out during the Miocene.

Microbrachis

During the Carboniferous Period – the Age of Amphibians – the ancestors of modern frogs, toads, and salamanders thrived. Some were large and heavily built, but others were small and well adapted to life in swamps and lakes.

Metamynodon

Microbrachis

Metamynodon had a stocky build and short legs. Rhinoceroses are perissodactyls, or "odd-toed" mammals. Although some perissodactyls have four digits, they never have the strong central pair of toes that the "even-toed" ungulates – the artiodactyls – have. *Metamynodon* had four short toes on the front feet and three on the back. Its large head sat on a thick neck. It had a short flattened muzzle, like a bulldog's, with large canine teeth sticking out from the mouth. Inside the mouth, there was a gap between the canine teeth and the heavy back cheek teeth. This may mean that *Metamynodon* used its tongue to move food from the front of the mouth to the back teeth for grinding and chewing.

Weight: 3.75-4 tons (3.5 tonnes)
Length: 15 feet (4.5 meters)
Found: North America
Lived: Oligocene

Microbrachis was a small lizardlike amphibian. It belonged to a group of amphibians called microsaurs, which means "little lizards," although lizards are reptiles. *Microbrachis* had a slim body, weakly developed limbs, and three fingers on each "hand." It probably spent most of its life near water, where it laid its eggs and caught most of its food – probably insects. Because of its small size, it could hide under rocks.

Weight: 6 ounces (170 grams)
Length: 6 inches (15 centimeters)
Found: Europe
Lived: Late Carboniferous

M

Mixosaurus

Although reptiles returned to live in the water during the Carboniferous Period, a greater invasion of the sea began in the Triassic. During this period, the ancestors of several present-day sea dwellers developed along with the first turtles. *Mixosaurus* was a very primitive fish-like ichthyosaur. It had a shorter snout and a longer, straighter tail than later ichthyosaurs. Its limbs were also less paddlelike.

Mixosaurus swam using its eel-like tail, which had long fins along the top and bottom. The streamlined body suggests that the animal could move quickly through the water, using its front limbs as rudders for steering. Like other ichthyosaurs, *Mixosaurus* was an agile hunter that preyed on fish and other sea animals. It would usually glide about slowly in search of food. Then, with powerful thrusts of its tail, it would propel itself toward its prey. Also like other ichthyosaurs, *Mixosaurus* gave birth to living young rather than laying eggs. It was unable to crawl onto land to lay eggs in the way that sea turtles do.

By the end of the Triassic Period, other ichthyosaurs had evolved and soon replaced *Mixosaurus* in the oceans of the world.

Weight: Not known
Length: 10 feet (3 meters)
Found: Europe, Asia, North America
Lived: Triassic

Mixosaurus

Moeritherium

Moeritherium

Moeritherium is thought to have been the ancestor of all the different types of elephants. It appeared some 53 million years ago in northern Africa. *Moeritherium* was only about the size of a pig or a pygmy hippopotamus. It was rather heavily built and had strong legs and large feet. It had a fairly long face with eyes placed quite far forward in it. The snout, or trunk, was short and flexible like that of the modern tapir. Inside the mouth, the cheek teeth were quite primitive, but were similar in some ways to those of the later elephants. The front teeth jutted forward. This probably helped the animal to tear at leaves and other plant material.

Moeritherium probably lived in swamps or along riverbanks, much as today's hippos do. Evidence exists to show that *Moeritherium* spread throughout most of northern and western Africa during the Late Eocene and Early Oligocene Periods. It may have been helped by a seaway, bordered by swamplands, across the continent.

Weight: Not known
Length: 3 feet (1 meter)
Found: Northern and western Africa
Lived: Late Eocene to Early Oligocene

M

Mosasaurus

This animal was one of the fiercest reptiles ever to hunt in the seas of the Cretaceous Period. The mosasaurs, or "Meuse-lizards," were first discovered in the White Chalk rocks of Holland and Belgium. They are distant relatives of lizards and snakes, and together they form a group of reptiles called the lepidosaurs.

Mosasaurus had a long serpentlike body and a big head with strong jaws lined with large conical teeth. A narrow wavy fin stretched the whole length of the body from the back of the head to the tail, which was flattened sideways. The tail propelled the animal through the water. Short rounded limbs were used for steering.

Mosasaurus was a powerful, agile swimmer. It hunted fish, turtles, and shellfish, including ammonites. Ammonites are extinct relatives of the octopus and squid. Several examples of their coiled shells have been found with holes punched through them by mosasaur teeth. During the Late Cretaceous Period, mosasaurs ruled the northern seas. They had replaced the ichthyosaurs and plesiosaurs as the dominant group of marine reptiles.

Weight: Not known
Length: 33 feet (10 meters)
Found: Europe, North Africa, North America
Lived: Late Cretaceous

Mosasaurus

Neanderthal man

Neanderthal man

Neanderthal man, known scientifically as *Homo sapiens neanderthalis*, was one of the earliest forms of modern humans. The Neanderthals were short sturdily built people. They had a broad face with a large protruding nose. Their eyes were set in high, circular, owl-like sockets. Above them were prominent brow ridges. Their forehead was flatter than that of a modern human, and the chin was weak. Another outstanding feature of Neanderthals was a marked swelling at the back of the head, or braincase, known as the "occipital bun."

Neanderthals lived mostly in caves, but they also built shelters of wood, elephant tusks, and skins. They used fire for warmth and for cooking. They shaped flints as ax heads, arrowheads, pointed spear tips, and meat cutters. From bone they made needles and carved ornaments. Neanderthals developed the sling and the bolas to hit and kill animals for food. They buried their dead in caves and performed rituals around the bodies and graves.

Neanderthal man lived in Europe until 35,000 years ago. He was replaced by humans that looked like modern man, called Cro-

N

Nothosaurus

Magnon man. It is likely that the two groups interbred and that the Neanderthals were assimilated into the other population.

Weight: 140 pounds (64 kilograms)
Height: 5 feet 7 inches (1.7 meters)
Found: Northern Hemisphere
Lived: Late Pleistocene

Neobatrachus

The skeletons of frogs and toads are delicate and have rarely been preserved in the fossil record. When the right conditions of soft mud and rapid burial occurred, however, beautiful fossils resulted. From them we have a record of *Neobatrachus*, an Early Jurassic frog. It was related to modern frogs and toads, and may well mark the split between them and the strange water-dwelling pipids and the primitive archaeobatrachids.

Neobatrachus had a broad head, strong front limbs with five fingers, and long back legs with five toes. It lived near the water, probably in damp undergrowth and vegetation. There it laid its eggs and fed on insects.

Weight: 3 ounces (85 grams)
Length: 4 inches (10 centimeters)
Found: South America
Lived: Early Jurassic

Neobatrachus

Nothosaurus

Nothosaurs were sea dwellers that seem primitive compared with plesiosaurs and ichthyosaurs. Although a long neck and tail gave them a slim outline, their bodies were not as streamlined as those of the other creatures. Also, their limbs still had fingers and toes, as land-dwelling reptiles did. *Nothosaurus* ranged in size from 1 to 20 feet (30 centimeters to 6 meters).

Nothosaurus, the "southern reptile," had a long head with nostrils perched on the front of the snout. The jaws bore many sharp teeth. The front ones were longer than the back ones. When *Nothosaurus* went hunting, the front teeth gripped tightly on struggling prey. The tail of *Nothosaurus* was flattened sideways and had a long deep fin along its top surface. The hind feet were webbed.

It is likely that *Nothosaurus* fed in the sea but crawled onto the land to lay its eggs. The fossilized skeletons of young nothosaurs have been found in beach and cave deposits. The nothosaurs were the near relatives of the larger-bodied plesiosaurs.

Weight: Not known
Length: 1-20 feet (30 centimeters-6 meters)
Found: Europe, Asia, North Africa
Lived: Triassic

O

Ophiderpeton

Small amphibians were common during the Carboniferous Period throughout Europe and North America. Over time, the limbs of many of these animals had become reduced in size or even lost altogether so that their bodies were snakelike or eel-like. *Ophiderpeton* had no limbs. The backbone of its snakelike body had more than 200 individual bones. The ribs were forked, a feature typical of the "aistopod" amphibians. Because *Ophiderpeton* had weak jaws, it is thought that the creature fed on water insects.

Ophiderpeton

In the latter part of the Carboniferous Period, or Coal Age, swamps and forests covered the Earth. Their later decay would help to produce coal deposits. The climate was warm and humid — ideal for amphibians. Insects were abundant and the fallen trunks of giant trees provided shelter from predators. *Ophiderpeton* would have been unable to protect itself from giants such as *Eogyrinus* or *Protogyrinus*.

Weight: Not known
Length: 2 feet 4 inches (70 centimeters)
Found: North America, Europe
Lived: Late Carboniferous

Osteolepis

Osteolepis was a lobe-finned fish that lived during the Devonian Period. It was an early relative of animals such as *Eusthenopteron* and *Dipterus*. *Osteolepis* had a slim body covered with heavy scales. It had a tapered snout and an uptilted tail. Behind the lower part of the head were paired fins, and along its back were two dorsal fins.

The skull of *Osteolepis* was covered by a number of bony plates. The eyes were placed forward and the mouth was long and slightly downturned. Sharp, pointed teeth lined the margin of the jaws. Like other lobe-finned fishes, *Osteolepis* was a hunter. It was a strong swimmer and chased other fishes for food. An osteolepid lived in freshwater, where it spent its entire life. Unlike its cousins the lungfishes, *Osteolepis* was unable to burrow into the sediment during periods of drought. And unlike *Eusthenopteron*, it did not rest or "walk" on its fins.

Osteolepis probably lived in upper waters of lakes and rivers. In comparison to other similar fishes and to *Dunkleosteus*, the giant placoderm, or "plate-skinned" fish of the Late Devonian Period, *Osteolepis* was quite small.

Weight: Not known
Length: 8 inches (20 centimeters)
Found: Europe, Asia, Antarctica
Lived: Devonian

Osteolepis

P

Oxyaena

Oxyaena

During the Paleocene and Eocene Epochs giant fish-eating birds such as *Diatryma* ruled the world. By the Middle Eocene, some 45 million years ago, various groups of large meat-eating mammals had replaced them. These carnivorous animals included the oxyaenids, catlike creatures that developed strong front legs and powerful shoulders. It is likely that these animals – of which forest-dwelling *Oxyaena* is one of the most important – relied more on the surprise leap than on a long chase to trap their prey.

Oxyaena was a small-brained, wolverine-sized cousin of *Patriofelis*. It had a short broad skull with powerful jaws. Massive shearing teeth were set into the jaws. The number of teeth was reduced from the number in primitive mammals, and the canine teeth were large and positioned at the front of the mouth. It was a formidable hunter.

Scientists place oxyaenids and the mongoose-like hyenodonts in the same group of early carnivorous mammals – creodonts. Animals in this group have a primitive type of cheek teeth. No oxyaenid animals survived the Eocene.

Weight: 66 pounds (30 kilograms)
Length: 2 feet 6 inches (75 centimeters)
Found: North America, Asia
Lived: Eocene

Palaeolagus

Rodents make up the most successful group of living mammals. They include squirrels, rats, mice, guinea pigs, and beavers. They are the gnawing animals, with sharp chisel teeth that cut and grind through both plant material and flesh. Most rodents eat parts of plants, such as nuts and fruit, but rats eat a variety of food.

Scientists used to think that hares and rabbits – lagomorphs – were rodents. There are a number of similarities between the two groups. It is possible, then, that they shared a common ancestor. But unlike rodents, no known lagomorph has had a long tail. The first hare appeared during the Late Eocene Epoch. By the Oligocene, there were many different kinds of hares living in the northern continents.

Palaeolagus was an Oligocene hare. Its head was about 2 inches (5 centimeters) long. Chisel-like front teeth made it look like a rodent. But, unlike the rodents, two additional teeth were located at the front of the upper jaw. A large gap, similar to that in modern rodents and hares, occurred between the chisel teeth and the cheek teeth.

Palaeolagus most likely lived on the grasslands that had begun to spread over central North America. From *Palaeolagus*, other groups of hares evolved during the Miocene and Pliocene Epochs. Modern hares and rabbits appeared during the Pleistocene.

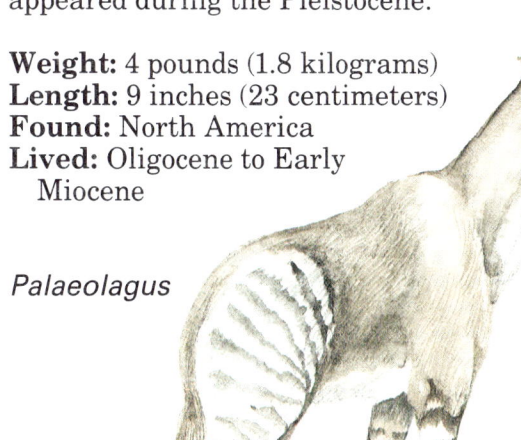

Weight: 4 pounds (1.8 kilograms)
Length: 9 inches (23 centimeters)
Found: North America
Lived: Oligocene to Early Miocene

Palaeolagus

P

Palaeomeryx

Deer appeared on Earth during the Miocene Epoch. Modern deer are, as they were then, browsing mammals that live in forests and forest glades. The males of true deer grow antlers, which they shed each year.

Palaeomeryx was an early deer that appeared in Asia about 18 million years ago. It and its relatives were probably the ancestors of modern deer. These early deer had low-crowned teeth, a typical feature of animals that feed on the leaves of bushes and trees. The horns of *Palaeomeryx* were simple compared with the branched antlers of modern deer. It is unlikely that *Palaeomeryx* – or its relative *Cranioceras* – both from the Miocene of Europe, shed their horns.

Palaeomeryx

Some of the close relatives of *Palaeomeryx* had very long canine teeth. In *Moschus*, a "tusk deer" that appeared during the Pliocene Epoch, the canines were like narrow tusks. *Moschus* bore no trace of either horns or antlers. Another tusked relative of *Palaeomeryx* was *Blastomeryx*, from the Miocene of North America. It is possible that these "tusked deer" used their front teeth to dig for roots or grind bark from trees.

Weight: Not known
Length: 2 feet (60 centimeters)
Found: Asia, Africa, Europe
Lived: Early Miocene

Panthera spelaea

Panthera spelaea

Among cats, the large "biting" kinds, such as lions, cheetahs, tigers, lynxes, and panthers, are the fiercest and most efficient flesh eaters ever to have walked the earth. Of these, the cheetah is the fastest runner of all living mammals, and the tiger the most feared. During the Pleistocene Epoch, huge cats lived in cold northern areas.

Animals such as the Cave Lion, *Panthera spelaea*, were savage beasts that could track and kill the giant Woolly Rhinoceros and even mammoths. The Cave Lion killed and ate its victims mostly on the open plains, but it sometimes dragged large carcasses back to its cave. The Lion and its pride spent much of their time there or nearby. Unlike the modern lion, *Panthera spelaea* had a rather long face and probably lacked a thick mane. It was built for stamina and strength, with a long body and long, strong legs.

Panthera spelaea and the other large biting cats evolved from *Pseudaelurus*, a leopard-sized meat eater that lived during the Miocene Epoch in Africa. Modern cats began to appear about 8 million years ago. At first they were in direct competition with the saber-toothed cats, but their speed and agility helped them survive, while the stocky *Smilodon* and *Thylacosmilus* died out.

Weight: 330 pounds (150 kilograms)
Length: 10 feet (3 meters)
Found: Europe
Lived: Pleistocene

P

Paranthropus robustus

This scientific name has recently been given to one of our ancestors. Until then, the name *Australopithecus*, or "southern ape," was used to describe this robust early human. Known from East Africa – Olduvai Gorge and Koobi Fora in particular – *Paranthropus robustus* is noted for its enormous cheek teeth and small front teeth. Apelike in appearance, *Paranthropus robustus* was larger and stronger than its close cousins *Australopithecus africanus* and *Australopithecus afarensis*.

In some ways *Paranthropus robustus* was very primitive. Family groups lived on the edge of rock slopes and forests. They ate both plants and fish, and they defended themselves by throwing stones or by beating with sticks. Adults stood slightly stooped but they were not "knuckle walkers" like the apes or the "oak ape," *Dryopithecus*. The remains of *Paranthropus* have been found in caves. It is likely that the bodies were dragged there by leopards, which pounced on the unsuspecting and unlucky creatures from overhanging branches.

Weight: 84 pounds (38 kilograms)
Height: 4 feet 6 inches (1.35 meters)
Found: Africa, Asia
Lived: Pliocene to Pleistocene

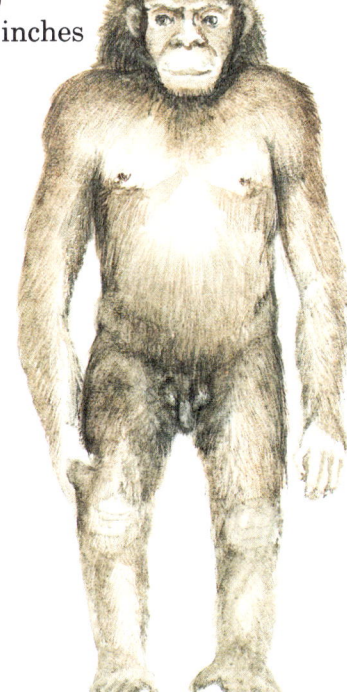

Paranthropus robustus

Peloneustes

Peloneustes

The "near lizards," or plesiosaurs, have been grouped into long- and short-necked kinds. The short-necked forms were called pliosaurs. *Peloneustes*, which lived in European seas, was an example of this group. It was about 10 feet (3 meters) in length and had a long head and a rounded body. The limbs were flipperlike, with the back flippers slightly larger than the front ones.

Peloneustes was a powerful swimmer. Unlike the long-necked plesiosaurs, the pliosaurs were long-distance swimmers. The front paddles moved with a strong downward and backward action. The back flippers were also used to pull the animal powerfully through the water. Similarly to the way birds fly through the air, *Peloneustes* "flew" through the water in search of its food. Squids, cuttlefish, and their distant cousins the ammonites were among the animals eaten by *Peloneustes*.

Other pliosaurs, such as *Kronosaurus*, grew to over 56 feet (17 meters) in length. *Kronosaurus* had massive teeth. Its head accounted for about one-quarter of its total length. This giant sea reptile of the Early Cretaceous Period lived in the seas of Australasia.

Weight: Not known
Length: 10 feet (3 meters)
Found: Europe
Lived: Late Jurassic

P

Phenacodus

Phenacodus

Phenacodus was a relatively small-bodied primitive ungulate. It had little hooves instead of clawed or nailed toes. In fact, it was one of the first of the hoofed mammals known scientifically as ungulates. *Phenacodus* looked like a medium-sized dog with slender proportions. Its face was long and the nostrils were perched on the tip of the snout. The animal's skull was fairly deep, and the brain was probably quite large. There were three toes on the back feet and four on the front.

Phenacodus is thought to have been a distant ancestor of the horses and tapirs. From the shape of the canine and cheek teeth, it is possible to determine that this early form was not specialized along the lineage of either of these animals. The large canine, or "dog," teeth are unusual. That has led some scientists to think *Phenacodus* was a flesh eater, although most believe it was a plant eater.

Phenacodus lived from 50-65 million years ago. It probably inhabited woodland glades or the edges of forests.

Weight: Not known
Length: 3 feet (1 meter)
Found: Europe, North America
Lived: Late Paleocene to Middle Eocene

Pholidogaster

Many ancient animals with backbones are hardly known because fossil skeletons are rare. There are many reasons for this, but the strongest is that the remains of some animals were fragile, and they were disturbed or destroyed before they could be buried or preserved.

This is certainly true of amphibians. The record of these animals is quite poor.

Among the Carboniferous amphibians was the first of the so-called anthracosaurs, *Pholidogaster*. The individual bones that made up the spine of an anthracosaur were unique, and the bones in the roof of the skull were also distinctive. *Pholidogaster* had a long body and tiny limbs. Its head was quite large and its body deep and rounded. It probably spent most of its life in water and used its tail for swimming.

Weight: Not known
Length: 3 feet 8 inches (1.12 meters)
Found: Scotland
Lived: Early Carboniferous

Pholidogaster

P

Phororhacos

Flightless birds appeared 65 million years ago. Many were gigantic flesh-eating creatures. The modern ostrich and emu are typical flightless birds. They have long legs and small wings.

Phororhacos lived during the Oligocene Epoch. It had long legs and a large heavy body like an ostrich does. Unlike the ostrich, however, *Phororhacos* had a big skull with a large and powerful beak. In some ways it was similar to *Diatryma* of the Eocene Epoch. But the skull was deeper and the legs were sturdier.

Phororhacos

Modern flightless birds are expert runners. Speed and strength enable them to survive on the open plains of Africa and South America. During the Oligocene, *Phororhacos* and its relatives were the main hunters in South America. Local carnivorous mammals, small and primitive, were no match for these huge birds. A blow from the beak or a kick from one of these birds would have knocked a small mammal senseless. Only when North and South America were connected did the rule of the flightless birds weaken. The spread of flesh-eating mammals led to the disappearance of many species. The advance of humans also caused the disappearance of the "elephant birds," or moas, of New Zealand. During the Pleistocene Epoch, some grew to more than 10 feet (3 meters) in height.

Weight: Not known
Length: 5 feet (1.5 meters)
Found: South America
Lived: Oligocene

Placochelys

The placodonts, or "plated-tooth" reptiles, appeared during the Triassic Period about 230 million years ago. They flourished during that period in Europe, North America, and Asia. They may have been related to the nothosaurs, and possessed a single opening in the skull high on each temple, behind the eye.

The placodonts lived much of their lives in the water. *Placochelys* was a rather primitive placodont. It lived on the seashore and searched for food in lagoons and on the sea floor. It had a long body and a long tail. Its head was rather short, with a strong, beaked snout. Inside the mouth powerful flat teeth lined the jaws. The beak was used to pry seashells from the rocks, and the flattened teeth crushed them. The front limbs were quite short and had webbed "fingers." *Placochelys* swam by using its finned tail to propel it through the water. The limbs were used for steering.

Another placodont, *Henodus*, looked like the sea turtle *Dermochelys*. It had a flat body covered by a bony shell. It also had a horny toothless beak and paddle-shaped limbs.

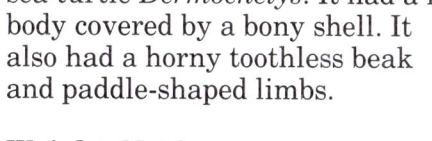

Weight: Not known
Length: 6 feet 6 inches (2 meters)
Found: Europe
Lived: Middle to Late Triassic

Placochelys

45

P

Placodus

A close cousin of *Placochelys* was the sea-dwelling reptile *Placodus*. Its head was larger than that of its placodont relative, and it had two main kinds of teeth. At the front of the mouth there were peglike teeth projecting in front of the jaw. The cheek teeth were large and flattened, making a strong, crushing plate with other teeth that covered the roof of the mouth.

Placodus had a short neck, a rounded body, and a long tail. The tail was flattened from side to side and probably had a long fin. The legs were quite strong and suited for walking. They also helped steer the animal when it swam.

Placodus lived along the shore of lagoons and shallow seas. It fed on oysters and clams in banks or on the edges of reefs. It pried the shells free with its peglike teeth and then crushed them to extract the soft flesh.

Unlike the plesiosaurs and ichthyosaurs, *Placodus* was not a strong swimmer over long distances. It probably spent most of its life on land and laid its eggs in shallow nests in soft sand.

Weight: Not known
Length: 7 feet (2.15 meters)
Found: Europe
Lived: Early to Middle Triassic

Placodus

Platybelodon

If you can imagine a rather small elephant with a face like a dump truck, then that animal would be *Platybelodon*. This "shovel-tusker" lived during the Miocene Epoch. Its lower jaw grew into a large flattened shovel, or scoop, and was covered by the flattened trunk, which extended in front of the upper jaw. *Platybelodon*, which developed from the smaller *Phiomia*, marked the peak of the development of the shovel-type mouth.

Platybelodon

Platybelodon has been described as the "bulldozer elephant," and this just about sums up its eating habits. *Platybelodon* fed in areas where lush soft plant life covered the ground. The front teeth on the lower jaw formed a sharp cutting ridge. The animal moved slowly forward, cutting the plants with the front edge of its mouth. Then, with its trunk or tongue, it pushed the food onto the cheek teeth for grinding.

Like other "shovel-tuskers," *Platybelodon* had two small tusks at the front of the upper jaw. These were directed forward and downward. They were the only defense a single animal had against large flesh-eaters. But it is likely that *Platybelodon* lived in herds to give it greater protection.

Weight: 4.5 tons (4 tonnes)
Length: 20 feet (6 meters)
Found: North America, Asia
Lived: Miocene

P

Plesiosaurus

This sea reptile lived during the Late Triassic and the Jurassic Periods. It was a member of the long-necked group of plesiosaurs that thrived throughout the world during the Mesozoic Era. *Plesiosaurus* had a relatively small head and short front limbs. Both these and the back limbs were shaped like paddles. Its body was barrel shaped, supported underneath by broad belly ribs.

Like other long-necked plesiosaurs, *Plesiosaurus* was an active, agile swimmer that hunted fish and other free-swimming animals in the open seas. Although *Plesiosaurus* had a strong tail, it swam, or "flew" through the water like modern sea turtles do. The long neck was used to rake across the water. The strong jaws and sharp-pointed teeth made short work of the unfortunate prey.

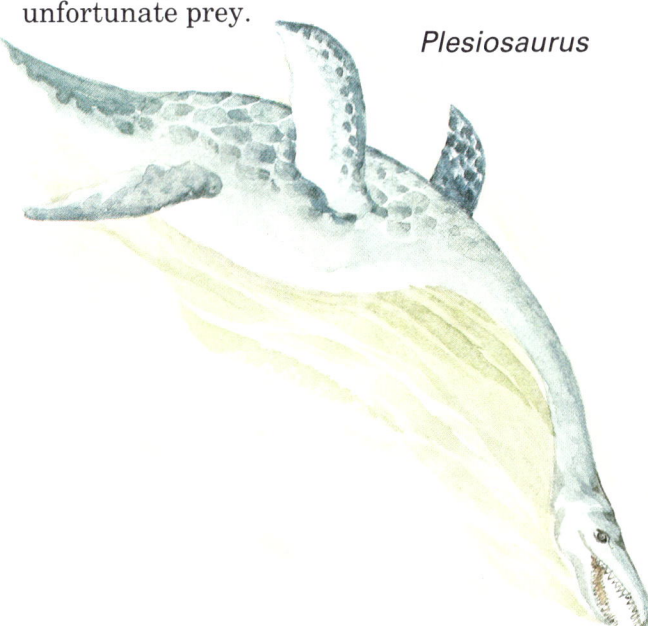

Plesiosaurus

Plesiosaurus was the smaller cousin of the gigantic *Elasmosaurus*. This larger animal's neck accounted for more than half of its total length. It had more than 70 separate bones. (Humans have 7.) *Elasmosaurus* grew to 40 feet (12 meters) in length.

Weight: Not known
Length: 10-13 feet (3-4 meters)
Found: Europe, North Africa, Asia
Lived: Late Triassic to Jurassic

Pleuracanthus

Pleuracanthus

Also known as *Xenacanthus*, this fish is an early example of a freshwater shark. The family of pleuracanths appeared in the Late Devonian Period about 355 million years ago.

Pleuracanthus had a long rather thin body with a shallow fin reaching from just behind the head to the tail. The paired fins were quite large and slightly rounded. The head was rather pointed, with a long thin spine poking upward behind the eyes. The long tail merged into the slim shape of the body. Like other sharks, the skeleton of *Pleuracanthus* was made not of bone but of cartilage. The remains of such animals are therefore quite rare and usually occur as impressions in mud-rich rocks.

The first known shark was *Cladoselache* from the Late Devonian Period in Europe and North America. *Cladoselache* may have looked much like the ancestor that gave rise to other sharks, including *Pleuracanthus*. Like other sharks, these animals ate flesh. *Pleuracanthus* probably fed on other fish and small amphibians.

Weight: Not known
Length: 2 feet 6 inches (76 centimeters)
Found: Europe, Australia
Lived: Carboniferous to Permian

P

Procoptodon

Procoptodon was a rather strange kind of early kangaroo with a short tail and a short rabbitlike face. It stood more than 10 feet (3 meters) tall. Like modern kangaroos, it was a plant eater and lived on the edges of forests and in areas covered by shrubs. It, too, was a marsupial, or pouched mammal.

Procoptodon

The ancestors of the kangaroos appeared in the Oligocene Epoch. In many ways, the kangaroos played the ecological role of the deer of North America and the zebra in Africa. Australia had separated from the rest of the southern continents earlier, and marsupials, including the kangaroos, evolved a variety of forms in isolation.

Procoptodon was successful during the Pleistocene Epoch. It had long legs, which enabled it to hop quickly over the ground, moving in huge leaps to avoid capture. The predator of this giant kangaroo was *Thylacoleo*, the marsupial lion. *Procoptodon* was related to other giant marsupials – such as *Diprotodon*, an early wombat – that lived at the end of the Pleistocene.

Weight: Not known
Length: 10 feet (3 meters)
Found: Australia
Lived: Pleistocene

Proganochelys

This animal, the earliest known turtle, was found in Triassic rocks of southern Germany. It had a strong shell protecting its body, as most modern turtles do. *Proganochelys* lived in marshes and ponds. It also had a beak similar to that of modern turtles, but it had teeth in addition. Ribs projected from the neck bones and it is unlikely that *Proganochelys* could pull either its neck or limbs into the shell for protection. The tail was quite long, with a club-shaped bone at its end.

The true ancestors of the turtles are unknown, but they may have been related to other reptiles with a solid skull roof.

Modern marsh turtles and land tortoises have varied diets. Terrapins feed on both flesh and plants. It is likely that *Proganochelys* ate the same variety of foods. Turtles and tortoises have few enemies except man. During the Jurassic and Cretaceous Periods turtles invaded the seas, and both turtles and tortoises spread throughout the world.

Weight: Not known
Length: 2 feet (60 centimeters)
Found: Germany, Thailand
Lived: Late Triassic

Proganochelys

P

Protosiren

Protosiren

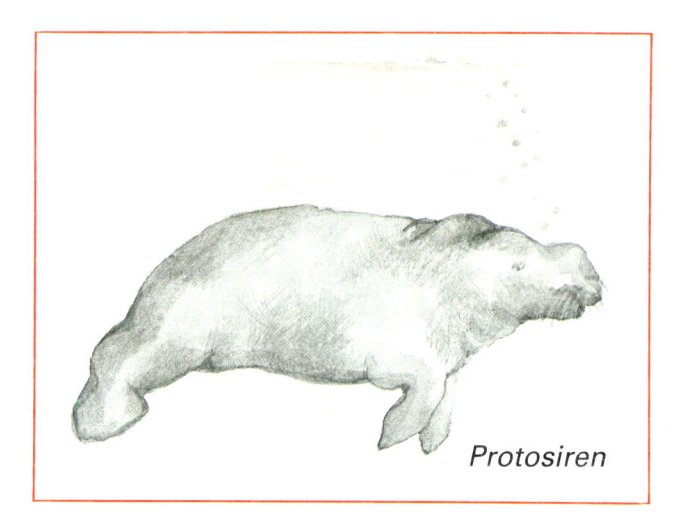

Sea cows, or sirenians, belong – as strange as it may seem – to the same group of mammals as the much larger elephants. Sea cows returned to life in the water during the Eocene Epoch. The link between sea cows and elephants and their ancestors is recognized because of the shape and nature of the cheek teeth.

Protosiren had quite a long head, similar to that of a walrus. Its front teeth were small, and its snout was swollen. *Protosiren* had a heavy body similar to that of a hippopotamus. But its front limbs were long, and it had no back limbs at all.

Protosiren lived in shallow coastal waters, as do the modern sirenians – dugongs and manatees. It probably stayed near the mouths of rivers, feeding on the lush foods that grew on the mud along the riverbanks. The first sirenians were found in the Eocene rocks of Egypt. In contrast to *Protosiren*, the heavily built *Palaeoparadoxia* from the Miocene had strong front and hind legs. This strange animal was a desmostylid – a relative of *Desmostylus*. Like *Protosiren*, however, *Palaeoparadoxia* lived quietly in coastal waters.

Weight: Not known
Length: 8 feet (2.4 meters)
Found: North Africa, Europe
Lived: Middle Eocene

Protosuchus

Protosuchus was one of the first crocodiles. Its fossil was discovered in Arizona. *Protosuchus* appeared about 200 million years ago. It probably shared the same ancestor as the dinosaurs – an archosaur, or "ruling reptile," similar to *Phytosaurus*.

Protosuchus had a long snout with the nostrils on the tip. It had strong jaws lined with sharp pointed teeth. The back and the long tail were covered with tough bony scales. Long legs, pulled closer to the body than those of other primitive reptiles, indicate that *Protosuchus* walked with a longer stride. It was quite a fast runner and an active hunter. It caught small reptiles and amphibians. *Protosuchus* divided its time between riverbanks and the water, in much the same way that crocodiles and alligators do today.

The skull of *Protosuchus* lacks many features of true crocodiles. By the Middle Jurassic Period, sea-dwelling crocodiles such as *Geosaurus* had appeared. These animals had paddle-type limbs, a tail like that of a fish, and no armor. They were very different in shape and size from their forerunner *Protosuchus*.

Weight: Not known
Length: 4 feet (1.25 meters)
Found: North America
Lived: Late Triassic to Early Jurassic

Protosuchus

P

Pteranodon

Pteranodon

Unlike early pterosaurs – "winged lizards" – *Pteranodon* had no tail and was toothless. It was also extremely large, with the wingspan of adults reaching 26 feet (8 meters)! Unlike a bird's wing, that of the pterosaurs was formed from a thin but tough sheet of skin stretched between the fingers of the hand and the knee of the back leg. In *Pteranodon* the fourth, or inner, finger was enormously long.

As in birds, however, the bones of *Pteranodon* were light and hollow, and the whole creature weighed less than 37 pounds (17 kilograms). The long bones of the arms were short and strong and provided a good attachment for the powerful muscles. It is unlikely that *Pteranodon* beat its wings to take off, but their huge surface area would have helped the animal to become airborne in the slightest breeze. Once off the ground, *Pteranodon* probably hovered and soared with the rising current of air.

The head of *Pteranodon* was unusual. It bore a large thin crest of bone 27 inches (68 centimeters) long and less than 1½ inches (4 centimeters) thick. The crest was lightweight and did not support strong muscles. It probably worked simply as a rudder, balancing the animal as it floated over the seas and rocky shoreline. Some bones of *Pteranodon* have been found far inland from the Cretaceous seas. It appears that *Pteranodon* may have been a scavenger, feeding on the carcasses of dead animals.

Weight: 36.5 pounds (16.6 kilograms)
Length: 9 feet (2.8 meters)
Found: North America
Lived: Late Cretaceous

Pterichthyodes

Also known as *Pterichthys*, this small "plated-skin" fish, or placoderm, lived during the Middle Devonian Period. Compared with other placoderms, such as *Dunkleosteus* and *Climatius*, it was primitive. But it was one of the earliest jawed fishes. *Pterichthyodes* lived on the sea bottom. It was a poor swimmer and spent most of its life searching for food on the soft bottom mud.

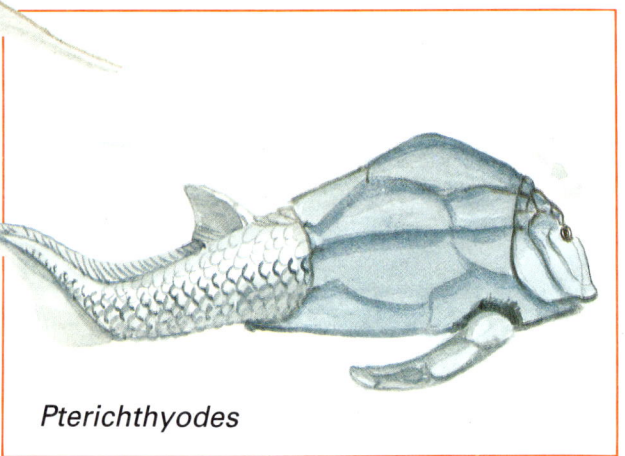

Pterichthyodes

Pterichthyodes was odd looking, with a flattened face and a boxlike head. The front part of its body was covered with an armor of bony plates. They were arranged in pairs, with the larger paired plates behind the mouth on both the upper and lower sides. On either side of the head, behind the mouth, were two backward-pointing "horns." They may have supported the animal in the mud. The rear part of the body and the tail were covered with small, tough scales. There was a strong fin behind the head shields. The tail was upturned, and the larger lobe of the tail fin was on the lower part.

Although *Pterichthyodes* is considered to be a jawed fish, its mouth was still quite suckerlike. The jaws were made up of small plates of bone that helped the mouth to open and close. Much stronger jaws developed in distant cousins – *Acanthodes* and *Euthacanthus*.

Weight: Not known
Length: 6 inches (15 centimeters)
Found: Europe
Lived: Middle Devonian

P

Pteroplax

Amphibians appeared during Late Devonian and Early Carboniferous Periods. *Pteroplax* dates from the Late Carboniferous, 290 million years ago. It is also known as *Eogyrinus*. It was large and eel-like, with small limbs and a long tail. It spent most of its life in water. Its back legs had small, webbed feet, but the tail was used most in swimming. The head was quite long, with many sharp teeth in both upper and lower jaws.

On land, *Pteroplax* was slow-moving and cumbersome. In water, however, it moved swiftly in search of food. It was the major predator and flesh eater in the swamps where it lived. Adult animals grew to 15 feet (4.5 meters) long. Few fishes or other amphibians were safe from them. It is difficult to think of such a large fierce amphibian, in comparison with its modest present-day descendants.

Weight: 550 pounds (250 kilograms)
Length: 15 feet (4.5 meters)
Found: Europe
Lived: Late Carboniferous

Pteroplax

Pyrotherium

When the skeleton of *Pyrotherium* was first found, scientists thought that the animal was an early elephant. Now, however, it is known to be a very different type of mammal that developed in South America when that continent was surrounded by the sea and isolated from northern and other southern lands.

Pyrotherium

Pyrotherium was a hoofed animal, or ungulate. It stood about 6 feet 6 inches (2 meters) tall at the shoulder. Its feet were very much like those of an elephant, but its body was long and the head strangely different. The snout was long and trunklike. Large ears and small eyes gave the animal a piglike appearance. Chisel-like tusks were present in both upper and lower jaws. *Pyrotherium* fed on plant material, using both trunk and tusks to hold and cut the food before it was pushed further into the mouth.

Many of the animals that lived during the Oligocene in South America were remarkably similar in shape to their northern cousins. *Pyrotherium* has been called a "pseudomastodon," or mastodon look-alike. Some resembled horses, others deer or rodents. Mostly they were more primitive than similar animals that had evolved in the north and failed to survive when the two landmasses were linked together 2 million years ago.

Weight: 2.75 tons (2.5 tonnes)
Length: 13 feet (4 meters)
Found: South America
Lived: Oligocene

51

Q

Quetzalcoatlus

The name of this huge pterosaur means "feathered serpent." It lived about 75 million years ago and was one of the largest animals ever to have flown. Discovered in Texas and later in Alberta, Canada, *Quetzalcoatlus* had a wingspan of 36-39 feet (11-12 meters). Like *Pteranodon*, it was basically a glider, soaring in the hot currents of air, called thermals, that rose up from the flat plains.

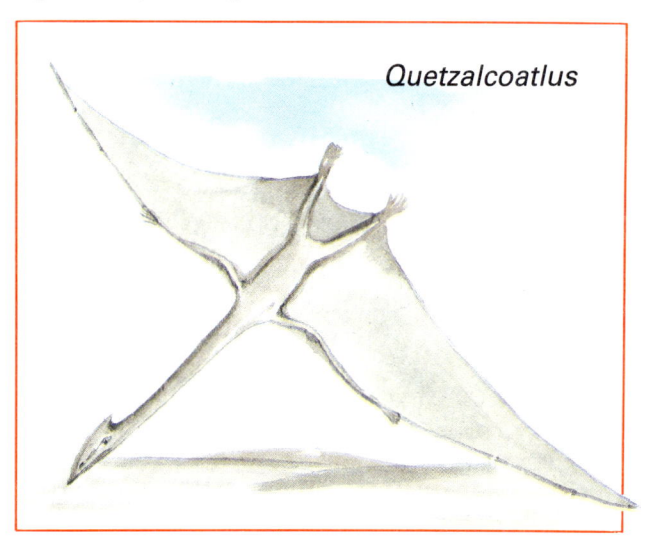

Quetzalcoatlus

Quetzalcoatlus lived farther inland than *Pteranodon* and more certainly fed on carrion – dead animals. *Pteranodon* was quite short-necked, but *Quetzalcoatlus* had a long neck and no crest. It behaved similarly to the modern vulture, gliding high over the ground waiting for an animal to die or be killed. Its survival depended on good eyesight, and it probably glided with its head bent toward the ground. Once it spotted a possible source of food, it swooped to the ground and ripped and gobbled up flesh until it was satisfied.

Quetzalcoatlus and *Pteranodon* were the last of the flying reptiles. At the end of the Cretaceous period they were replaced by several groups of modern birds.

Weight: 190 pounds (86 kilograms)
Length: 13 feet (4 meters)
Found: North America
Lived: Late Cretaceous

Ramapithecus

Ramapithecus

Ramapithecus was a chimpanzee-sized animal that lived from 7-14 million years ago. Most scientists today believe it to be an ape, a distant relative of the living orangutan. *Ramapithecus* walked mostly on its back legs and lived on the edges of woodlands. It lacked the large canine, or "dog," teeth of the "oak ape," *Dryopithecus*, and had a jaw and tooth structure similar to early humans.

The development of an upright posture was important during the evolution of humans. Many of the features necessary for upright posture may have originally developed in apes like *Ramapithecus*, which spent most of their time hanging vertically from branches. Later this vertical posture could have been modified for two-leg walking on land, the way it was in *Australopithecus* and early species of our genus, *Homo sapiens*.

Weight: 66 pounds (30 kilograms)
Length: 4 feet (1.2 meters)
Found: Europe, Africa, Asia
Lived: Miocene

S

Rhamphorhynchus

This long-tailed pterosaur lived during the Late Jurassic Period, some 140 million years ago. It was small compared with its cousins *Pteranodon* and *Quetzalcoatlus*. It was probably a more active flier – it probably beat its wings like a bird and did not soar high above the ground. *Rhamphorhynchus* had a long snout, and its long teeth interlocked when the jaws were closed. This indicates that the creature fed on fishes, which is not surprising since it lived near the lagoons and swamps that fringed the Jurassic coastline.

Sordes pilosus, or the "hairy filth" pterosaur from the Jurassic of Russia, was a close relative of *Rhamphorhynchus*. It was covered with a furry down, which helped the animals to maintain a constant body temperature.

During the Late Jurassic short-tailed pterosaurs appeared. They soon replaced the long-tailed forms such as *Rhamphorhynchus*.

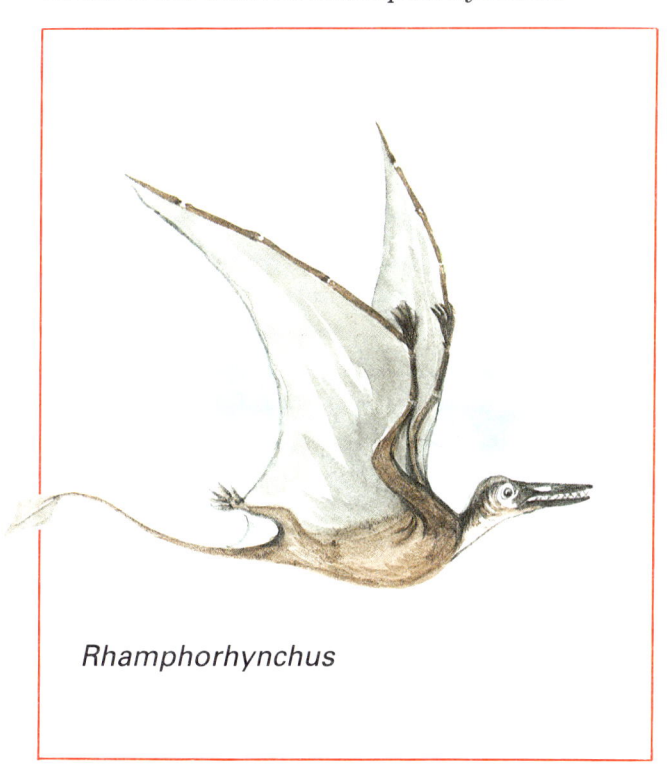

Rhamphorhynchus

Weight: Not known
Length: 2 feet 2 inches (66 centimeters)
Found: Europe, Africa
Lived: Late Jurassic

Saltoposuchus

This creature was a lightly built archosaur, or "ruling reptile." It lived about 210 million years ago and may be counted as one of the ancestors of the dinosaurs. *Saltoposuchus* was a bipedal – two-legged – reptile. The back legs were long, in contrast to the very short and quite weak front legs. The animal had a long tail, and its body balanced over the hips.

Saltoposuchus

Saltoposuchus was a flesh eater, and many sharp pointed teeth lined its jaws. Small reptiles and amphibians were its diet. Small armor plates arranged in two distinct rows ran down the back. These provided some protection against larger meat eaters.

Weight: Not known
Length: 3 feet 9 inches (1.15 meters)
Found: Europe, North America
Lived: Late Triassic

S

Scutosaurus

Primitive reptiles appeared during the Late Carboniferous Period, and many of them were small. By the Late Permian, large heavily built creatures such as the plant eater *Scutosaurus* had evolved. It had a sizable skull that was

Scutosaurus

covered with bony lumps. Some individuals also had hornlike growths. The jaws were strong and the teeth leaf-shaped and saw-edged. Small teeth also covered the roof of the mouth.

Scutosaurus was a slow, cumbersome creature. The bones of the legs, shoulders, and hips were massive, and the chest was deep and rounded. Fortunately its large size presented a challenge for a would-be predator. *Scutosaurus* spent much of its life feeding, its sharp teeth slicing easily through tough twigs and stems. Unlike many of the other reptiles of its group, *Scutosaurus* stood upright and walked with a longer stride than sprawlers such as *Limnocelis* or *Labidosaurus*.

Weight: 484 pounds (220 kilograms)
Length: 8 feet (2.4 meters)
Found: Europe
Lived: Late Permian

Seymouria

As with many fossils, the name *Seymouria* is taken from the name of the place where the remains of this animal were found. In this case the place was Seymour, Texas. *Seymouria* is an important fossil because it marks a major stage in the attempt by amphibians to advance onto dry land. In some ways the skeleton of this amphibian resembled that of a reptile. The skull had fewer bones than that of other amphibians, the jaws were shorter, and a distinct notch marked the position of the ear. The spine was strong, and the long bones, hands, and feet were more like those of a reptile than those of an amphibian. *Seymouria* was very near the lineage that led to the first reptiles.

Seymouria

Young animals closely related to *Seymouria* had gills, a typical amphibian feature. *Seymouria* laid its eggs in water and, when hatched, the young went through a similar change to that which takes place when a tadpole changes into a frog. Many larger amphibians were eventually replaced by water-dwelling reptiles, and their numbers began to decrease at the end of the Paleozoic Era, 225 million years ago.

Weight: Not known
Length: 2 feet (60 centimeters)
Found: North America
Lived: Early Permian

S

Sivatherium

This gigantic giraffe lived about a million years ago during the Pleistocene. Unlike the modern giraffe, *Sivatherium* was heavily built, with a thick neck; a large, horned head; a long face; and a rather pointed snout. The horns were massive and branched, and the animal never shed or lost them. Large males stood 7 feet (2.2 meters) tall at the shoulders.

In contrast to the African giraffe, *Sivatherium* had shorter legs, a deeper chest, and stronger, more muscular shoulders. The back of the animal sloped quite markedly toward the tail.

Sivatherium browsed on leaves and twigs on woodland edges and on shrub-covered plains. Its enemies included the large biting cats.

Sivatherium

Weight: Not known
Length: 10 feet (3 meters)
Found: India
Lived: Pleistocene

Smilodon

Of all the saber-toothed cats, *Smilodon* is perhaps the best known and most spectacular. It was also the most successful. Its remains have been found in both North and South America, in rocks from the Pleistocene Epoch.

The skull measured 12 inches (30 centimeters) in length and was fitted with long, daggerlike dog teeth. These were used for stabbing prey. Large powerful jaw and neck muscles gave the animal the ability to drive the teeth downward with great force. The first stabbing action was all-important because *Smilodon* was unable to hold on to its prey for very long. It is likely that the first bite was to the neck and to the blood vessels.

Powerfully built with strong limbs and muscular shoulders, *Smilodon* was a fierce enemy. It most likely fed on the large mastodons that roamed the northern lands during the Pleistocene.

Smilodon

In South America the appearance of *Smilodon* must have had some impact on the large slow-moving hoofed animals. The evolution of the more agile biting cats may have led to the disappearance of *Smilodon* as the fast-paced pursuit of fleet-footed prey became more important.

Weight: Not known
Length: 5 feet (1.5 meters)
Found: North and South America
Lived: Pleistocene

S

Stenaulorhynchus

This was one of the earliest "beak-headed" reptiles, or rhynchosaurs. These animals get their name from the down-curved beak shape of the end of their upper jaw. Most members of this group, such as *Scaphonyx*, were heavy-bodied, with a broad deep skull and a prominent beak. This creature fed on plant material that it crushed with the aid of rows of toothplates.

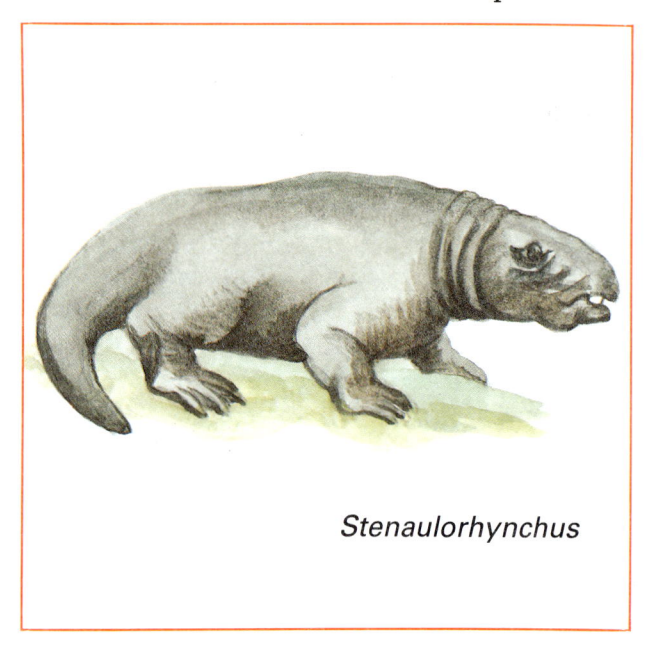

Stenaulorhynchus

Stenaulorhynchus was more lizardlike than *Scaphonyx*. It was a direct ancestor of the modern *Sphenodon*, a small creature that is known only from islands off the coast of New Zealand. "Beak-headed" reptiles thrived throughout the Triassic and Jurassic Periods and then became extinct. The peak of rhynchosaurian evolution was during the Middle Triassic Period, when numerous forms lived in areas such as East Africa, Brazil, and Argentina. These animals were able to spread more easily during this period because the southern continents were joined to form one large landmass called Gondwanaland.

Weight: Not known
Length: Not known
Found: East Africa
Lived: Middle Triassic

Steneosaurus

Steneosaurus

During the Triassic Period seas covered much of the world. Our knowledge of land-dwelling animals is therefore limited to specific areas or groups that had adapted to a life in water. Crocodiles were mainly coastal or riverbank dwellers, although *Geosaurus* was one kind that lived in the sea.

Steneosaurus was a long-snouted crocodile that fed on fish. It probably lived at the mouths of rivers and swam with the use of its tail. *Steneosaurus* was one of the first members of the mesosuchian group of crocodiles – a direct ancestor of all modern crocodiles. Its skull, about 30 inches (75 centimeters) long was strong, with many sharp pointed teeth lining the jaws. A club-shaped end of the upper jaw was typical of this creature.

Steneosaurus laid its eggs in a shallow nest. The developing young were protected until they hatched. Once they were out of the egg and nest, they were prey to a number of other reptiles, including the fast-flying pterosaurs, such as *Rhamphorhynchus* and *Dimorphodon*.

Weight: Not known
Length: 16 feet 5 inches (5 meters)
Found: Africa, Europe, Madagascar
Lived: Jurassic

T

Tanystropheus

This reptile, which lived during the Middle Triassic Period, was most unusual – its neck was longer than the combined length of its body and tail. The body was similar to that of a modern lizard, only larger, but the neck was more than 10 feet (3 meters) long. The individual bones of the neck, the vertebrae, were longer than those of any other animal of its size. Some vertebrae measured over 12 inches (30 centimeters).

The long neck suggests that *Tanystropheus* spent much time in the water. The animal probably could not run fast on land. *Tanystropheus* may have fished in rivers and coastal waters, where a long neck would have let it probe below the surface to catch fish, small reptiles, and amphibians. Some scientists have suggested that it lived in the sea because its bones have been found in marine deposits. However, the animal had normal limbs and a rounded, relatively short tail – signs of a poor swimmer.

There is a doubt about the true relationship of *Tanystropheus* to other reptiles. It was probably closer to nothosaurs and placodonts than to lizards or snakes, as is sometimes thought.

Weight: Not known
Length: 20 feet (6 meters)
Found: Europe, Middle East
Lived: Middle Triassic

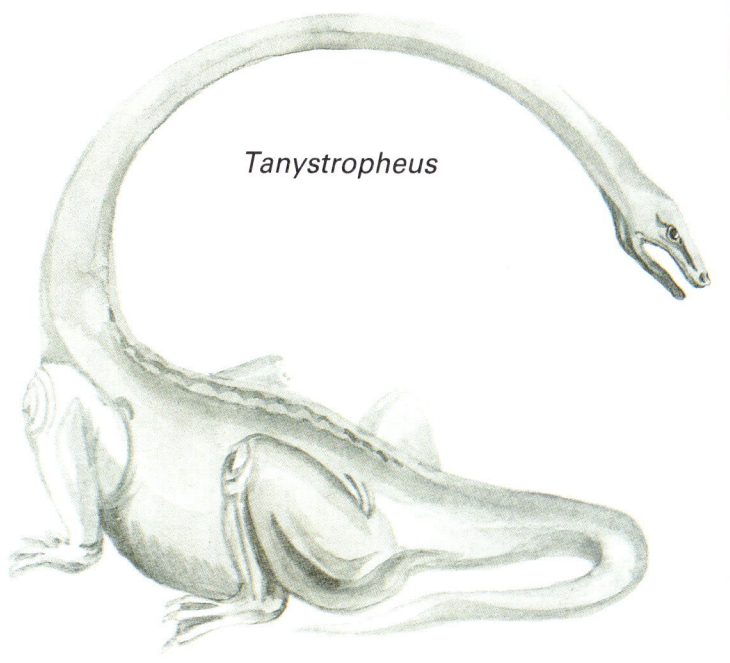

Tanystropheus

Thylacocinus

During the Pleistocene Epoch the marsupials of Australia appeared in a variety of forms. But most of them were descended from opossumlike ancestors. Among the new species was *Thylacocinus*, the Tasmanian "wolf." It was a pouched mammal that ate flesh. *Thylacocinus* was a member of one of the basic marsupial groups and had primitive teeth. It was wolflike in build, and similar to some of the meat-eating marsupials that lived in South America during the Pliocene and Pleistocene.

Thylacocinus

Thylacocinus competed for its food with *Thylacoleo*, the marsupial "lion." *Thylacoleo* had tusklike front teeth and most likely fed on both flesh and plant material. These animals may have filled the same ecological role as the lion and the hyena in Africa today. During the Pleistocene, *Thylacocinus* also lived in New Guinea. In more recent times this animal was confined to Tasmania.

Weight: Not known
Length: 3 feet (1 meter)
Found: Asia, Australia
Lived: Pleistocene to 20th century

T

Thylacosmilus

Although this great cat was not related to the saber-toothed, or stabbing, cats, it did have huge daggerlike teeth. *Thylacosmilus* was a flesh-eating marsupial, or pouched mammal. Like the saber-toothed cats it stabbed at its prey and relied on an instant kill for its food. Like many saber-tooths – such as *Smilodon* – *Thylacosmilus* had long bony flanges on the lower jaw that guided and protected the daggerlike sabers when the jaws were closing.

An adult *Thylacosmilus* was about the size of a leopard. It roamed the plains of South America and fed on large hoofed creatures such as *Toxodon*. *Thylacomilus* filled the same hunter-killer role as *Thylacocinus* did in Australia.

At the end of the Pliocene, large biting cats such as *Smilodon* invaded South America. They were more agile, efficient hunters, and they soon replaced the less agile marsupial forms. The young of *Thylacosmilus* were helpless when they were born. They had to crawl into their mother's pouch and suckle until they were large enough to walk, run, and hunt on their own. This may or may not have played a role in the extinction of *Thylacosmilus*.

Thylacosmilus

Weight: 154 pounds (70 kilograms)
Length: 4 feet (1.2 meters)
Found: South America
Lived: Pliocene

Toxodon

Fossils of this large, hoofed mammal have been found only in South America, where it appeared some 6 million years ago. It was probably a plant eater. *Toxodon* was the size of a rhinoceros, with short legs and broad three-toed feet. The head was rounded and had a flattened snout. The front teeth were rather large – in fact, the name *Todoxon* means "bow-tooth." The head was supported on a short neck and hung low, in front of the shoulder blades. A high back ridge and a deep chest were other features of this animal.

Toxodon was one of three famous fossil mammals discovered by Charles Darwin on a visit to South America. His discovery was helped because a skull of the animal was the target for several young boys who were throwing stones. It was later found that *Toxodon* was one of the few animals that spread northward into Central America during the Pleistocene Epoch. Together with the tree sloth and the capybara, *Toxodon* spread northward, inhabiting the Central American land bridge.

Toxodon

Weight: 5 tons (4.5 tonnes)
Length: 10 feet (3 meters)
Found: South and Central America
Lived: Pleistocene

Triconodon

Triconodon

The first mammals appeared during the Triassic Period. For many millions of years, mammals were dominated by reptiles, particularly dinosaurs. Throughout the Mesozoic Era, from 65-225 million years ago, mammals were small, often tiny, creatures that slept during the day and searched for food at night. Because of their size and their delicate skeletons, early mammals are poorly known – many only from their teeth.

Triconodon was a member of an early group of mammals that lived during the Jurassic and Early Cretaceous Periods. It was the size of a house cat, and it was probably a flesh eater. Its teeth were sharp and pointed, and most had three high points, or cusps. *Triconodon* lived in fear of the meat-eating dinosaurs, such as *Compsognathus* or *Coelurus (Ornitholestes)*. In turn, however, it was feared by smaller mammals, reptiles, and amphibians. Unlike some of its close relatives, *Triconodon* did not eat insects.

Weight: 6.5 pounds (3 kilograms)
Length: 1 foot 6 inches (45 centimeters)
Found: Europe
Lived: Jurassic

Trogonotherium

Trogonotherium was a gnawing mammal, or rodent, that lived during the last Ice Age. Its remains have been found only in Europe. It was a relative of the modern beaver, and more distantly of squirrels. *Trogonotherium* had high-crowned cheek teeth for grinding food, as present-day beavers do. Modern beavers live in water, and it is likely that many of their ancestors did the same.

Trogonotherium

Trogonotherium and its American cousin, *Castoroides*, were very large, however, with *Castoroides* growing to the size of a young bear. The head of *Trogonotherium* was large with massive chisel-like teeth at the front of both upper and lower jaws. This ancient beaver also had a long body and tail. The hind legs were shorter than the front ones.

The first beavers appeared during the Oligocene Epoch. *Stenofiber*, a primitive beaver from the Oligocene, Miocene, and Pliocene Epochs in Europe, is thought to have lived in complicated burrows, called "devil's corkscrews."

Weight: Not known
Length: 6 feet 6 inches (2 meters)
Found: Europe
Lived: Pleistocene

T

Tylosaurus

The mosasaurs, or "Meuse-lizards," were the major hunter-killers of the Late Cretaceous. They were sea dwellers with paddlelike limbs. Their body was long and streamlined with a pointed head and long narrow tail. They grew to 26 feet (8 meters) in length and flourished in the waters of the northern Atlantic and the southern Pacific oceans.

Tylosaurus fed on fish and free-swimming mollusks, including squids, cuttlefish, and their shelled cousins the ammonites. Such small animals stood no chance when *Tylosaurus* was feeding. It was a powerful, agile swimmer, and the huge jaws with large, pointed teeth would snap quickly to make a kill. *Tylosaurus dispar* from the Cretaceous marine rocks was one of the largest of all mosasaurs. *Globidens*, a close relative, had flattened teeth that are thought to have been used to crush clams.

Weight: Not known
Length: 26 feet (8 meters)
Found: America, New Zealand
Lived: Late Cretaceous

Tylosaurus

Uintatherium

To our eyes this rhinoceros-sized creature from the Eocene Epoch would have looked bizarre. Its head was covered with bony knobs. Most adult animals had two or three pairs of these lumps, with the larger, longer ones above the eyes and alongside the nostrils. In male animals the canine teeth took the form of powerful tusks.

Uintatherium

Uintatherium was the giant of the Eocene. Its body was bulky, with thick legs and broad feet, like those of an elephant. It lived in forest glades and fed on twigs and leaves.

The natural enemies of North American Eocene plant eaters was the doglike *Synoplotherium*. Although this beast hunted in packs, it is unlikely that it would have attacked an adult *Uintatherium* in its prime. Old animals and young calves may have been targets, but fully grown males or females were too large and too strong. *Synoplotherium* more likely preyed on the small horse *Hyracotherium* or the tapir *Helaletes*. Both of these animals lived at the same time as *Uintatherium*.

Weight: 2.25 tons (2 tonnes)
Length: 13 feet (4 meters)
Found: North America
Lived: Eocene

Z

Ursus spelaeus

Bears are among the largest of living meat-eaters. *Ursus spelaeus* – the "Cave Bear" – was a very large animal that survived the fierce winters of the Ice Age by hibernating in warm caves. One cave in Austria is famous for the number of skeletons that it contained. Scientists have counted over 30,000 from this one site, and it is thought that many of the bears died during their long sleep.

Ursus spelaeus and ancient humans competed for the same homes and probably often battled each other to the death for that reason. Neanderthal man was a skillful hunter, but he showed his respect for the power of the Cave Bear by burying its head in the floor of his cave home. It is likely that Neanderthal man thought of the bear as a totem of strength and protection.

Ursus spelaeus

Other cave dwellers of the Pleistocene Epoch included the Cave Lion and hyenas. During the winter the sleeping bears would have been a good source of food for these animals.

Weight: 880 pounds (400 kilograms)
Length: 5 feet 3 inches (1.6 meters)
Found: Europe
Lived: Pleistocene

Zalambdalestes

Zalambdalestes

Zalambdalestes was a small, insect-eating mammal that lived in Mongolia during the Late Cretaceous Period. Its skull was about 2 inches long and less than an inch high, and contained a small primitive brain. The teeth in the upper and lower jaws had many sharp points that interlocked with one another when the jaws closed, the way they did in other insect eaters.

Zalambdalestes was similar in structure to the oldest insect eaters, animals that were probably the most primitive placentals – mammals whose babies develop inside the maternal sac. For millions of years none of the insect eaters evolved into even medium-sized animals. The insect-eating shrews are the smallest of all modern mammals, and they have changed little since the Cretaceous Period. Their tiny size and retiring habits probably have contributed to their survival in a world where so many other kinds of animals have come and gone.

Weight: Not known
Length: Not known
Found: Mongolia
Lived: Late Cretaceous

Animal History

Paleozoic Era — Age of Fishes and Amphibians						Mesozoic Era — Age of Reptiles			Cenozoic Era — Age of Mammals					
Cambrian Period	Ordovician Period	Silurian Period	Devonian Period	Carboniferous Period	Permian Period	Triassic Period	Jurassic Period	Cretaceous Period	Tertiary Period				Quaternary Period	
									Paleocene Epoch	Eocene Epoch	Oligocene Epoch	Miocene Epoch	Pliocene Epoch	Pleistocene Epoch	Holocene Epoch
(began 570 million years ago)	(began 500 million years ago)	(began 440 million years ago)	(began 395 million years ago)	(began 345 million years ago)	(began 280 million years ago)	(began 225 million years ago)	(began 190 million years ago)	(began 136 million years ago)	(began 65 million years ago)	(began 54 million years ago)	(began 38 million years ago)	(began 26 million years ago)	(began 7 million years ago)	(began 2 million years ago)	(began 0.01 million years ago)

Fishes

Amphibians

Reptiles

Birds

Mammals

Humans

62